*continued . . .*

"The premise of this book—that parents can help their kids develop the entrepreneurial mindset they need to be successful—resonated deeply with me. This is a must-read for parents."
—Kevin Ryan, chairman and founder of Gilt, MongoDB, Business Insider, and Zola

"Our children will live in a world in which entrepreneurial individuals who can take risks and lead others amid uncertainty will capture outsized returns. This is a guide to help you raise children who will excel in that world."
—Kyle Jensen, PhD, Yale School of Management

# Raising
# *Can-Do* Kids

Giving Children the Tools to Thrive
in a Fast-Changing World

## Richard Rende, PhD
## & Jen Prosek

A TarcherPerigee Book

**tarcher**perigee

An imprint of Penguin Random House LLC
375 Hudson Street
New York, New York 10014

First trade paperback edition 2016

Library of Congress Cataloging-in-Publication Data
Names: Rende, Richard, author. | Prosek, Jennifer, author.
Title: Raising can-do kids : giving children the tools to thrive in a
fast-changing world / Richard Rende PhD, Jen Prosek.
Description: First trade paperback edition. | New York : TarcherPerigee,
2016. | Hardcover edition published in 2015 by TarcherPerigee. |
Includes  bibliographical references and index.
Identifiers: LCCN 2016022289 (print) | LCCN 2016027289 (ebook) |
ISBN 9780399168963 (hardcover) | ISBN 9780399168970 (paperback) |
ISBN 9780698153035 (ebook)
Subjects: LCSH: Parenting. | Parent and child. | Personality development. |
Social skills in children. | Children—Conduct of life. | BISAC: FAMILY &
RELATIONSHIPS / Life Stages / School Age. | PSYCHOLOGY / Developmental /
Child. | FAMILY & RELATIONSHIPS / Parenting / General.
Classification: LCC HQ769 .R435 2016 (print) | LCC HQ769 (ebook) | DDC 306.874—dc23

Printed in the United States of America
1   3   5   7   9   10   8   6   4   2

Book design by Laua K. Corless

RICHARD:

For Cheryl, Iliana, and Carlo (RIP)


JEN:

To my parents,
who shaped the entrepreneur in me

To my husband,
who enabled my entrepreneurial success through our partnership

To my daughter,
who drove this quest, which became this book

And to Dan Jacobs, my original partner in business,
who is the reason I became an "accidental entrepreneur"

# CONTENTS

Introduction ............................................................ ix

**1** | Wired for Exploration ................................ 1

**2** | Primed to Innovate ................................... 39

**3** | Raising Optimists ...................................... 73

**4** | Opportunity Seekers ................................ 101

**5** | Doers ......................................................... 131

**6** | People Skills ............................................. 161

**7** | Serving Others ......................................... 189

| Epilogue ............................................. 213

Acknowledgments .............................................. 219

Notes and Resources ......................................... 223

Index ..................................................................... 241

# INTRODUCTION

Before we launch you into this book, we think it would be helpful to tell you a little about how it came about. In 2012, one of us—Jen, a successful entrepreneur—contacted the other of us—Richard, a child development researcher—to explore partnering on a book. Our conversation, however, quickly turned into a discussion of the uncertainty we were both feeling as parents. While we all want to raise our kids to be "successful"—is there a more ubiquitous phrase these days when it comes to kids?—both personally and professionally, it's just not clear how we should do that, because the world our kids will enter someday is becoming increasingly unpredictable.

We talked about some of the basic concerns we keep hearing about. Kids can have the most outstanding academic and extracurricular profile imaginable and *still* get rejected by a lot of colleges, as the number of applicants keeps growing while the number of available slots doesn't change much. They can have an Ivy League degree and not get the job they want, and a college degree certainly doesn't guarantee immediate employment.

If they do manage to land that job, they might find that it's either going to morph in unpredictable ways, or that it may even disappear. If the social scientists are right, we are fast becoming a nation of free agents who bear full responsibility for engineering our careers and our lives. The availability of good jobs and fulfilling careers won't be a given for the rising generation. Many of today's most prestigious companies and professions won't even exist. How do we prepare our kids for *that*?

Jen related that, given present-day conditions, she wanted her daughter to learn throughout childhood the skills she would need to successfully navigate the world's unpredictability. It seemed less important that her daughter know about a specific field or notch a specific credential; rather, she needed to build skills such as adapting, improvising, learning, persevering, and spotting opportunities. We agreed that the old paradigms of parenting for success are becoming increasingly obsolete. If we want our kids to thrive in that unpredictable world that awaits them as adults, we can't just hyperfocus on pushing them as hard as possible through the predictable path of schoolwork, exams, and extracurricular activities. There has to be something more we can do to prepare them for a future that we can't entirely envision.

Jen suspected that raising kids to become more like *entrepreneurs* would help. Entrepreneurs typically make their way in the world with no road map to guide them; they must motivate and inspire themselves, applying their passion and creativity to create success for themselves and value for others. People had often asked Jen if her parents had done anything special in raising her and her brother, since both had gone on to work for themselves (Jen as the founder and CEO of an international communications business, her brother as an independent artist and writer). The more Jen thought about it, the more she realized that she and her brother *had* been encouraged at home to do things like explore, be creative, be optimistic, seek out opportunities, make their own choices, and know how to get along with others. Jen realized that the very skills and outlook she experienced as a child were exactly the strengths she brought to her business *and* the capabilities she wanted to instill in her daughter. It wouldn't matter whether or not her daughter eventually wanted to become an entrepreneur—rather, her thinking was that she would be well equipped to pursue her own successes by being *entrepreneurial*.

Jen put it to Richard: Was it reasonable to think that parents could help their kids cultivate entrepreneurial skills? And was Jen right in thinking that cultivation of entrepreneurial skills would benefit *all* kids, even those who didn't particularly aspire to start their own companies or pursue business careers?

Richard agreed that Jen's thinking resonated when we think about kids growing up right now. He had enjoyed a long career as an academic developmental psychologist and educator, having conducted many studies on how the family environment influences children's development. From a scientific standpoint, what he liked about Jen's approach was that it was "road tested"—it was demonstrably true that entrepreneurs gravitate to and thrive in a changing, unscripted world. Further, entrepreneurs tend to do what they love *and* pursue professional success—essentially the goal that *all* parents have for their kids. Richard knew from his previous work that the kinds of entrepreneurial skills Jen was thinking of *were* realistically attainable for all kids, and that you didn't have to be a budding "business type" to benefit from them. He believed, as Jen did, that parents can't definitely assure their children's future happiness and success, and they can't assume that the world will prove a hospitable place either. What they *can* do is give their kids the strongest possible platform so that *kids can do for themselves*— now, tomorrow, and decades from now. That "can-do" spirit was exactly what kids today will need to take on uncertainty to create their own success.

Jen proposed that she and Richard collaborate to write a parenting book that mobilizes the latest child development research to help parents nourish entrepreneurial skills in their kids. Richard enthusiastically agreed and was especially excited about focusing rigorously on "evidence-based practices." It's fashionable to throw out all kinds of ideas about parenting, but what matters is the *evidence*. As Richard explained, research never delivers an exact "answer" to a question. What scientists do, at any given moment, is step back and consider the big picture that emerges from research, both the long-standing findings and the new trends. There are always ambiguities, and there is always more research that could be done, especially when we're talking about new experiences for children. That said, academic research is powerful because it takes what we know, right now, and arrives at a conclusion that is *best* supported by all the evidence. Those kinds of conclusions are what Richard wanted to present to parents.

Jen agreed, and the idea for *Raising Can-Do Kids* was born. Afterward, we spent two years researching and writing the book. Our first step was to draft a short list of entrepreneurial skills or traits that not only conformed to what is known about entrepreneurs but that also connected well with decades of child development research. Our initial list wasn't exhaustive, but it captured core elements of the entrepreneurial experience, and best of all, it gave rise to a range of evidence-based practices for parents. We utilized this list by performing in-depth interviews of some two dozen entrepreneurs across a range of professions, asking these individuals to reflect on how certain skills or traits had impacted their lives (for example, in their childhood, in the careers), and in some cases how they had influenced their own behavior as parents. Our goal was not to extract "proof" from all these talented and successful people, but rather to get real-life stories that illustrated how entrepreneurial skills were put to use in the world. Where appropriate, we dipped into secondary research on entrepreneurs to further illuminate what the main entrepreneurial skills were, and how entrepreneurs put them to good use.

We eventually refined our list to focus on seven skills or traits that span core domains of development—cognitive, personal, and social. These skills became our framework for looking at the scientific literature and thinking about suggestions for parenting strategies, along with reflecting on popular writings about parenting that help reflect current parenting culture. We focused on two related cognitive skills that parents might easily cultivate in babies, toddlers, preteens, and teens—*exploration* and *innovation*. Among researchers a consensus seems to exist that children innately possess the ability to explore and innovate, but that they need to cultivate these skills in particular ways as they grow in order to develop to the fullest. All too often, the thinking goes, our educational system fails to do this sufficiently, and our kids wind up lacking what they will need to succeed. It's worth noting that the concepts we review converge with what many identify as "twenty-first-century skills" all kids will need to thrive as they make their way across developmental stages and eventually go out into an uncertain world.

An additional three personal traits jumped out at us as we thought more deeply about entrepreneurs. *Optimism* was a big one: By thinking about how it benefits entrepreneurs as they run their companies, we came to understand a number of ways it could be a protective and powerful skill for children. A similar thing happened when we thought about a quintessential entrepreneurial trait: *risk-taking*. Much has been written about how our culture may be raising children to avoid risk, and how such coddling might hamper their development. In interviewing entrepreneurs, we discovered that they tend not to take extravagant or foolhardy risks for their own sake; rather, they strategically pursue opportunities that at times *may* carry some level of risk. This surprising behavior helped us shape a useful definition of what constitutes productive or reasonable "risk-taking" in children, which we reframe as "opportunity seeking."

A third personal skill—*industriousness*, or put more simply, being a "doer"—also stood out as we interviewed entrepreneurs. Entrepreneurs tend to take on "dirty jobs" and develop a habit of doing for themselves; this stands in contrast to allegations lodged by cultural critics and others that today's kids are being raised to be "entitled."

Beyond cognitive and personal skills, our research highlighted how useful two specific social skills are as entrepreneurs build new businesses. *Likeability* helps entrepreneurs mobilize teams and build relationships, and it also turns out to be an asset for all children as they progress in their development; meanwhile, diminished likeability can restrict a child's academic success and eventually damage their professional trajectories. Finally, we embraced a concept frequently discussed in business circles, the idea that *serving others* is not only personally fulfilling for individual professionals, but a pathway to success in almost any domain. The parenting research bears out how important this is for children as well.

Throughout the book, we suggest concrete actions or techniques readers can adopt so as to parent their kids more effectively. Don't feel you need to follow our suggestions slavishly. Instead, just use them as starting points. Not every moment of a parent's life can be artfully crafted to nurture optimal development, but child development research *does* help identify parenting behaviors that allow our kids to develop their innate abilities to the fullest. Some of our suggestions are derived from cutting-edge research, others from scientific findings established and reestablished over decades—we step back and identify the most helpful takeaways that represent current thinking in child development. We hope you use this book creatively, taking the ideas and tips and putting them into practice in your own way, with a bit of confidence that these will serve you and your kids well. Bear in mind that researchers who study kids continually enjoy learning more about what kids can do and take pleasure in uncovering their capabilities. We anticipate you will have fun applying some of what you discover in this book.

An entrepreneurial can-do spirit is ultimately what childhood, and development, is all about. Kids must adapt to an ever-changing and uncertain landscape in school and on the playground, and they must be able to rise to challenges and navigate inevitable disappointments. While "can-do" has a retro feel to it—and, in fact, much of our book reveals new thinking about the current importance of a number of "old-school" traits—there is also a freshness to the concept that cuts to the core of the challenges our kids will face in the future. Jen attended a conference in December 2014 on emerging market trends, and the leader, a futurist named Edie Weiner, introduced a concept so powerful it stopped Jen in her tracks. Weiner proposed that we are moving from a world of "have and have-nots" to a world of "can and can-nots." Career success in the years to come won't stem as much from who you know or your academic credentials (what you *have*); it will depend simply on whether you have the right skills—most of all, the ability to learn, grow, and reinvent yourself or what you *can do*. Individuals who can adapt to the constantly changing needs of the marketplace and get from A to Z without a road map will survive, thrive, and find happiness. Entrepreneurs are natural "cans." And our kids will become "can-do kids" if we successfully pass along to them some elements of the entrepreneur's experience and skills, especially when coupled with the evidence-based practices supported by current research.

As parents, we want our kids to develop a set of skills that will position them well to define and find both happiness *and* career advancement. While our first conversation about this book focused on the uncertainty our kids will face, we have come away from the experience feeling good that raising can-do kids is certainly a satisfying way to prepare them for this exciting life that awaits them.

# 1

# WIRED FOR EXPLORATION

Considering the technological proficiency of young children today, we might assume that these digital natives are better prepared for success than prior generations. A toddler may possess skill sets that many adults didn't acquire until, well, adulthood, and will acquire new proficiencies beyond anything we might imagine. But as tech entrepreneur Dan Harple observes, there is one thing dangerously missing in children's formative experiences—something that prior generations had in spades. "Today's kids have different 'boundary conditions' than we did growing up in the sixties," Harple notes. "We had more unbound freedom. We just went out to play, unsupervised, with no goals for developing competencies. We would flip swing sets over and bounce off of trampolines. I saw things changing in the eighties, the transition to overstructuring and formalizing our kids' activities. When I became a parent, I resisted a lot of those pressures. Kids need to be able to run and explore."

It's perhaps surprising that a techie like Harple would think back so longingly for his low-tech childhood. And keep in mind, Harple is not your ordinary techie. We could spend a whole chapter detailing his contributions as an innovator and entrepreneur. He pioneered Voice over IP (VoIP), streaming media, and interactive screen sharing/shared whiteboards in the early 1990s. He was the cofounder, chairman, and CEO of InSoft, which merged with Netscape Communications Corporation in 1995 and provided, among other things, standards for real-time media to the Internet and the first real-time web platform (which millions of people use daily for web video). Harple has founded a number of other companies, including Context Media (acquired by Oracle in 2005) and gypsii. Harple is currently the managing director of Shamrock Ventures BV as well as a Sloan Fellow at the Massachusetts Institute of Technology, where he serves as entrepreneur in residence (EIR). And for all these impressive tech credentials, Harple fondly recalls the role of free time and exploration in his childhood, and also posits that today's youth require it as well—despite their prowess with gadgets.

A father of five children, Harple walks the walk. While his kids certainly had opportunities to learn technology when they were growing up, they were not always on the computer, and they had ample time for a range of unstructured experiences. "When I was the CEO/chairman of Context Media, my office was a bit larger than it needed to be. One corner of my office had a small dome tent. There is where my kids came and played while I worked. They brought their papers and crayons and toys and 'worked' from my office." Harple's kids could observe the comings and goings of people and whatever else was happening in the office; they enjoyed the unstructured time, a chance to play and absorb new experiences.

Harple liked bringing his kids to work because he remembered spending time with his own dad, an electrical engineer. "My dad repaired musical equipment—amplifiers and organs. I would just hang with him in the shop and watch him work. Sometimes he'd ask me to find something, say, a thirty-watt resistor, which gave me a chance to explore all the pieces of equipment that were around. I'd also observe all the musicians who would come by to drop off and pick up their equipment. I just soaked up a lot of experiences that would shape what I did later in life."

## All Work, No Play = Childhood?

Harple's recollections of his youth speak to a concern expressed by many child development advocates: Children don't get enough time these days for free play. Evidence is increasingly suggesting that parents do not sufficiently appreciate the role free play has in helping build a number of cognitive and personal skills vital for personal and professional achievement. In 2007, the American Academy of Pediatrics (AAP) published a detailed report on data suggesting that free play has been declining over the past two decades in both home and school. A primary example was the decrease in recess time. In the summer of 2014, public radio station KUOW Puget Sound reported that eleven public schools in Seattle had restricted recess to twenty minutes a day or less. Four years ago, only one school was adhering to this practice. This is especially disconcerting because long-standing research has repeatedly shown that increased recess time leads to *better* academic performance. Bear in mind that another report by the AAP (published in 2013) focused specifically on *preserving and restoring* recess time in the early school years and the importance of allowing for sufficient time (for example, more than thirty minutes) for kids to fully engage in activities. Yet we continue to hear news that schools are retracting recess time.

Step back in time and think about what kindergarten was like for you. Chances are, it was a half-day program. We spent time playing and doing art projects in addition to foundational introductions to reading and math. By contrast, it's not unusual to hear about kindergarten classrooms in 2014 that focus heavily on "academics" and dismiss not just recess but other key features of traditional early childhood education, like arts and crafts.

Forget for a moment about the data, research, and theory. Doesn't the idea of a five-year-old not having the chance to go outside and play through the course of a seven- or eight-hour day sound strange? How about canceling the school play in kindergarten because more time is needed to prepare five- and six-year-olds for college? The latter actually happened in the spring of 2014 in a school in Elwood, New York. A letter was sent out to parents explaining that it was more important to focus on reading, writing, and problem solving to ensure success in college and beyond. Again, a far cry from the kindergarten many of us grew up with.

It's important to remember that typical kindergarten activities such as playing and putting on cute plays aren't just tangential, fun things for children to do. They are primary ways children learn and develop multiple cognitive abilities and academic readiness. An authoritative review of the benefits of play, published in *Psychological Bulletin* by Dr. Angeline Lillard and colleagues at the University of Virginia, concluded that giving young children *freedom to choose from a range of hands-on activities* confers the most benefits on cognitive development in the earliest years of schooling—as compared to highly structured classrooms that focus on providing top-down instruction from teachers. Children of all ages learn best by using multiple senses and by being experiential. Kids need to be active explorers of their world.

> Kids need to be active explorers of their world.

Discussion abounds in the press and social media about whether overstructuring our children's lives substantially restricts time for free play and exploration at home as well. The journalist Josh Levs has proposed parental anxiety as the primary factor behind such overstructuring. Parents, it seems, are concerned that kids will fall behind if they don't stay competitive in academics, sports, dance, and any other domain that might lead to success in adulthood. At the same time, many parents such as Dan Harple realize that kids are not being given the chance to develop their own passions for activities like sports or music.

We don't fault parents for wanting their children to be successful, and for striving to provide all possible opportunities to help them get there—in fact, we agree with that goal. The issue is how we achieve that goal. We get that some structured activities *are* productive. But future success will also require a wide range of experiences, and the formative years lay a foundation for kids, one that allows them as adults to navigate opportunities and challenges. Keep in mind, the ability to adapt to a changing environment—to be entrepreneurial and proactive in the face of change—is becoming more important than ever in today's economy. Catherine Clifford, writing on Entrepreneur .com, notes that "[i]t used to be that entrepreneurs were the renegade cowboys out in Silicon Valley. Nowadays, you have to be an entrepreneur just to get and hold a job." She cites factors like the business appeal of hiring independent contractors and outsourcing jobs, among other trends. Jen sees ample evidence of these trends every day in her work. She further notes that some young employees are able to learn on the fly and improvise, while others aren't. One of Jen's prerequisites for hiring employees is their possession of what she calls an "adaptation aptitude." And as the science tells us, the best way to gain such an aptitude is through exploring new situations and becoming comfortable navigating the unknown.

According to a paper published in *Evolutionary Psychology*, uninhibited free play during childhood lays the groundwork for adaptability. The fundamental lack of structure in play allows children to explore without boundaries—and when play includes other kids, it introduces unpredictability that requires and inspires adaptation. As kids make up a game, they learn to roll with new rules that they define in the moment. The authors of this paper suggest that this ability to adapt to change in childhood is associated with success in adulthood. Children *need* to be entrepreneurial when they go out into the world. Otherwise, they're just not prepared.

> Children *need* to be entrepreneurial when they go out into the world.

Imagine your daughter excels in science throughout high school, goes to a great college, goes on to a high-powered graduate school, gets a PhD, and is considered one of the great new minds in the field. What will happen next? Well, she will have to hope that funding levels in the biomedical sciences are strong enough to permit some institution to offer her a job. And then what? She'll be asked, in short order, to begin to develop grant applications that will fund not just her research, but her salary and benefits, too. That's going to require all kinds of entrepreneurial skills that will aid her as she navigates funding trends, grant mechanisms, and changing priorities of funding agencies. And this need to adapt and improvise will be the case for the rest of her career in order to function at the highest level as a scientist.

In the years ahead, *all* kids will have to be entrepreneurial if they are to truly make it. One place to help—while they're still in diapers—is to make them naturals at exploring their environment.

## Openness to Experience

In personality psychology, the tendency to explore, manipulate, and discover is captured by the trait known as "openness to experience." Dr. Colin DeYoung, an expert researcher in this area, has described openness to experience as "cognitive exploration," which includes "the ability and tendency to seek, detect, comprehend, utilize, and appreciate complex patterns of information, both sensory and abstract." This trait has been shown to predict success in the arts, sciences, and other disciplines—including entrepreneurial success. Drs. Hao Zao and Scott E. Seibert analyzed the findings of twenty-three research studies (using meta-analysis, a statistical technique to summarize an overall pattern of findings) and concluded that entrepreneurs, as compared to managers, scored "significantly higher" on openness to experience.

Curiosity, exploration, and discovery are core components of an entrepreneurial mindset. Jen suggests that entrepreneurs live with their "radar screens" on. They are willing not only to experience the world—but to actively survey everything going on around them. They like to absorb as many data points as possible because it gives them an edge. For Jen, everyday experiences offer stimuli she can utilize in her practice of public relations. During a ride in a taxi, chance phrases offered by the driver may trigger a new thought that could serve a client well. Entrepreneurs discover the advantages of paying attention every minute of the day, and those "radar screens" are always primed to detect signals that could be put to good use.

It may seem logical to think that some people are simply born with this trait. Personality traits, in general, are assumed to be somewhat genetic in nature. So is it possible that openness to experience is driven *exclusively* or even *primarily* by our DNA? Could entrepreneurial types just have a higher "dose" embedded in their genome? Hardly. The overarching conclusion from many "genetically informative" studies (for example, natural experiments that compare the similarity of identical and fraternal twins) is that openness to experience reflects a moderate amount of influence from genes—about 50 percent. Now, a statistical estimate such as this probably means a little less than you would think. It doesn't mean that, for a given person, half of his or her tendency for openness to experience stems from their genes and the other half derives from their environment. The truth is, some people are rated high for openness to experience, some are rated low, some are in between— and the guess is that genetic makeup tells only half of the story. But even that is speculative, as the types of statistical models scientists use to calculate heritability don't actually identify genes but rather try to model the cumulative effect of many hypothetical genes. And the bottom line from this work is that while genes contribute to behavioral tendencies, the environment matters a whole lot as well.

All this may sound complicated, and it is. So let's repeat the basic point: Openness to experience is not something only *some* people are born with. Lived experience *does* matter. Yes, experientially as a parent, you may observe that your child is more or less open to experience. But that doesn't mean you can't or shouldn't try to cultivate this trait anyway and encourage your child to always have their radar screens on, ready to detect interesting things in their world.

## Babies Use Their Radar Screens, Too

Babies come into the world wired (in the neuroscience sense) for exploration. Like entrepreneurs, they have their "radar screens on" to search for meaningful signals in the everyday noise of their environment. Babies are also intuitively equipped to seek out the *right kind of information*—data that their brains are best suited to handle. They can search through a nearly infinite amount of information to focus on stimuli their brains crave. Because of this, they are equipped to make sense of the world in surprisingly sophisticated ways. And having some insight into how they do this can help you, as a parent, appreciate their need for exploration as you promote essential skills in that first year of life.

Consider the visual phenomenon researchers call the "Goldilocks Effect." Like Goldilocks, babies have a sweet zone of what's "just right" when they are looking at things. One study utilized sophisticated technology to track seven- and eight-month-old babies' eye movements in response to varying levels of complexity in the types of stimuli presented to them. If something is too simple, it will not hold babies' attention for very long and they will stop looking at it. If something is too complicated, they will also lose interest very quickly. But if something has just the right amount of information—not too simple, not too complicated—then a baby will lock in and explore it. The point here is that you don't have to go crazy buying things to stimulate a baby. The world itself holds plenty of interest, as long as babies are given sufficient opportunity to find their "just right" level of processing.

You can see newborns' ability to function as explorers in other ways as well. Newborns can recognize a voice in the first weeks of life, and even in the first days. How do we know this? Selective movement is the key—the baby will turn its head one way or the other to try to find the origins of that recognizable voice. Another example is the rooting reflex: Stroke a newborn's cheek and its head will turn in that direction as a preparation to eat. In a few short weeks this won't just be a reflex; babies will start turning selectively to their food source (bottle or breast), indicating that knowledge about the "outside world" has formed.

What makes discovery especially compelling for babies is that while the world they encounter is blurry and fuzzy and ever-changing, it also offers enough continuity so as to seem a fairly predictable place. Processing a stream of new stimuli as well as repeatable patterns, babies naturally explore while also feeling secure. A similar balance between predictability and novelty is also something that every entrepreneur needs in order to make her business sustainably innovative. A business lacking in repeatable patterns, one that is purely innovative, winds up being unstable, while one with too much patterned behavior lacks innovation. Entrepreneurs like Jen don't have to teach themselves from scratch how to sustain this balance. Rather, they only have to relearn something they already learned on a very basic level during the first few months of life.

## Cultivating Exploration from Birth On

If babies are more sophisticated cognitively than we think, how might we begin to cultivate their exploration early on? One thing to try is to stick your tongue out at a newborn or very young baby. Many of them will stick their tongue out in response. While researchers have debated the meaning of "tongue protrusion" in newborns for decades, recent well-designed research has confirmed that they are imitating adults. This may sound trivial, but it's not. It's actually quite a cognitive achievement in which selective perception (aimed toward the human face) is translated into motor control (sticking out the tongue) in order to support a social interaction. That said, even if a baby doesn't imitate the act, you are still getting into the habit of giving a baby interesting things to look at and perhaps respond to. You are reinforcing—even in the first days of life—the inherent tendency to explore.

The same principle holds for other behaviors that pique the interest of babies. Try to elicit the rooting reflex by lightly stroking a baby's cheek; the baby is likely to turn its head toward your finger in response. Talk to your baby as you walk around the room, and see when they start to track your voice. Create your own actions to get a response. You will feel a rush as your baby starts to flex their competencies. And any developmental expert will tell you that these are the core ways that infants begin to learn and integrate information in their environment—and, in fact, begin to realize that the world is an interesting place.

## Faces Versus Screens

You have undoubtedly heard about the importance of "face-to-face interaction" in the early years of life. There's a good reason for this. Babies have a "selective bias" toward the human face—they prefer to look at a face over any object. In fact, given the chance, they like to analyze it. One experiment studied how intensely babies read the face as part of learning language. Researchers found that four-month-olds focus on the eyes, six- to eight-month-olds zero in on the eyes and mouth, eight- to ten-month-olds go for the mouth, and twelve-month-olds focus on the eyes.

Why? For the youngest babies in the study—the four-month-olds—the eyes are the logical way of connecting with an adult. But a few months later, they also look at the mouth, where the sounds come from. The mouth becomes the sole target after that—now at eight to ten months—as the focus on the sound becomes intensive.

Why would a twelve-month-old go back to eyes? The four-month-old doesn't connect the mouth to sounds yet, but the twelve-month-old has all that figured out and is capable of processing language *without* looking at the mouth. That's not interesting anymore. The parent's eyes, however, are a source of additional information for the twelve-month-old, who is connecting what is being said to what the eyes are telling them.

This is an extraordinary amount of cognitive exploration that is happening and changing in *just the first year of life*. The age differences further support what we've been arguing—babies are wired to explore, but they need *ample opportunities* to engage intensely and continually search out what is most relevant to them. This is the basis for the phrase "face-to-face interaction" featured so prominently in messaging by pediatricians, psychologists, and developmental experts. It is meant quite literally. Babies *need* to study the face. It gives them (at varying ages) consistently interesting information that is "just right." The face is fascinating because it is dynamic in real time and it provides enough range of complexity to serve as an endless source of stimulation.

This is why child development researchers worry about screen time during infancy. Experts want to be sure that babies are getting as much human interaction as possible, and excessive screen time interferes with the face-to-face exposure babies need. Babies won't use their emerging sensory abilities and developing cognitive exploration skills to full capacity if they are focused on a screen. As advanced as tablets have become, screens are just not going to provide optimal stimulation for a baby. It won't provide that magical mix of intriguing yet digestible visual information that yields those "just right" moments of discovery that can change from month to month.

Think about how complicated it would be to program content on a tablet that would simulate all of the things the human face does. The range of emotions that you display, the nuances your face brings, all of the interplay between the eyes and mouth—no single interaction with your baby is ever exactly the same as another. As a test, sit down and play with any program on a tablet you might show a baby and compare that to watching yourself talk in the mirror, using a range of tones and emotional expressions. There's simply *more* you will see in that mirror. This is not to say that screen time is inherently harmful (though some will make that claim); the key is that screen time should not *replace* dedicated face-to-face time between parent and baby.

This discussion about face-to-face interaction and screen time in infancy is certainly not new. It is, however, more relevant than ever. The changes we're seeing now year to year are more dramatic than previous technology trends that took *decades* to unfold. Common Sense Media (CSM) is a nonprofit advocacy group that provides research on media use in children. CSM has been tracking, via nationally based surveys, changes in children's media use over the past few years; they issued reports on this data in 2011 and 2013. As described by Vicky Rideout, research director for CSM, the changes they observed during this two-year period have been unprecedented—primarily driven by increased access to media thanks to mobile technology. Consider some of these key findings:

» In 2013, 75 percent of kids (ranging in age from birth to eight years) had access to mobile devices, up from 52 percent.

» Smartphones are still the most common device (63 percent, up from 41 percent), but tablet ownership is five times higher (8 percent to 40 percent).

» The percentage of kids who've used mobile devices has nearly doubled (38 percent to 72 percent), and average daily use of mobile devices has tripled, from five to fifteen minutes a day.

As of 2014, nearly 40 percent of babies are using smartphones or tablets before their first birthday. Importantly, CSM has also shown that this increase in newer mobile technology usage is *not* accompanied by decreases in older technology; across the age groups, TV time continues to go up as well. For babies, this includes "secondhand" TV, or a TV that is on "in the background" although the baby is not sitting in front of it.

What do we make of all this? Is screen time for babies and toddlers advisable? Are there advantages to it? Should we be worried? In 2013, the American Academy of Pediatrics (AAP) issued new guidelines (the first change in more than a decade) recognizing that screen time has become dominant in the lives of families, children, and even babies. Child development experts now advocate for providing an appropriate balance between "passive" and "active" screen time. Passive screen time for a six-year-old would be watching a TV show, whereas active screen time would be doing a math problem on a tablet or other device. Both types are part of children's lives today, but it's important to know the difference and *especially* important to limit passive time.

One important recommendation has not changed. The AAP has continued its long-standing recommendation that pediatricians discourage screen exposure for children less than two years of age. We've been through this before. Television, video games, laptops were *all* proclaimed either unhealthy or nonoptimal for children before eventually becoming accepted by parenting experts. Yet something is different here. We used to have a lot of time to learn about new technology; research on the television was conducted for *decades* with few changes in the medium and its use. Over the past few years, the appearance of devices in the hands of babies and their parents has occurred with startling speed—to the point where we're on the verge of families being connected to technology 24/7. We've all seen babies with smartphones in malls and restaurants. Some strollers now come equipped to support an iPad for a baby. There has been, and always will be, the inevitable flood of educational claims about how certain software or games can increase reading and math skills. Will babies growing up with mobile devices turn out smarter and more cutting edge than prior generations? Scientists don't know; they haven't had the chance to study the new technology's impact.

Here's what we do know: Face-to-face interaction between a parent and baby is paramount, and no other type of stimulation can simulate that process or deliver equal cognitive, emotional, and social benefits. Face-to-face interaction is the foundation for exploring the world in the first year of life.

## Make Interaction Count

How can you best optimize interaction time with your baby? One easy thing to do is to get in your baby's face—literally. A baby needs proximity to your face to soak up all the information it conveys. Talk to baby while you are holding him or her, and position yourself so you are face-to-face. Notice how they become locked into you. As they get older, get down on the floor and let them sit on you, again face-to-face. You get the idea here. As babies develop, make sure you find a way to let them study and enjoy your face. Think about games like peekaboo—there is no better way to promote face-to-face interaction, and you and baby will have a great time doing so. Also, don't be shy about being animated and using a lot of expression. Facial expressions such as joy and surprise and wonder provide a complex and delightful palette for your baby to explore. A primary reason babies find your face so interesting is that it is a primary tool for emotional bonding. The same holds, of course, for your voice. All those inflections that correspond to the range of positive emotions you can express provide another stream of stimulation that is engaging and rewarding to a baby.

These techniques work best when you can devote *undistracted time* to your baby. Set aside times when you won't use technology—even the background noise of a TV can become competing white noise. Think about it this way: If you can find fifteen minutes every hour to deliberately interact face-to-face with your baby, you will establish a routine that allows you and baby to engage with each other in cognitively important ways, and you'll still be able to go about daily life. Of course, feeding time, diaper time, and other caretaking activities will also provide natural opportunities for interaction—and it's a great idea to capitalize on those as well. You can use the time when your baby is napping (or even looking at a screen) to catch up on your own screen time. You'll find that you feel more comfortable—and less guilty—about exposing your baby to screen time when you know you are deliberately setting aside time for face-to-face interaction.

## Position Your Baby for Exploration

More than ever, developmental researchers are embracing the idea that cognitive development is driven by movement. Babies, toddlers, and children *learn more* when they move and directly manipulate objects in their world. But until babies can move on their own, they are dependent on others to provide the opportunities for them to actively engage with their surroundings. You can, therefore, promote cognitive exploration by becoming mindful of how you position your baby. Drs. Michele Lobo and James Galloway provided a group of parents/caregivers with three weeks of training in "enhanced handling and positioning" of their babies, who were two months old. These enhanced behaviors included supported sitting and standing as well as the prone position (on the tummy). These babies were then examined in conjunction with a second group of babies whose parents/caregivers did not participate in the three-week training program. The hypothesis was that enhanced positioning would encourage the development of muscle tone and motor skills that lead to cognitive exploration.

Results were immediate. Over the next few months (from three to five months of age), the "enhanced" group showed notable advances in a number of indicators of motor development, like reaching for objects. The benefits did not stop there. Up to a year later, those babies continued to show advances in motor development—including object manipulation and transfer of objects from one hand to the other. Interestingly, many of the parents/caregivers who received this training reported that it affected how they interacted with their infant over the next year. They became attuned to the idea that babies' exploration is supported by motor development, and that by encouraging and fostering motor development, they can facilitate their baby's cognitive growth.

Another study makes the links between motor development and cognition even more explicit. Here babies who ranged from 4.5 to 7.5 months were brought into a laboratory where researchers observed how they visually and manually explored play objects. The goal was to see if these babies would know to look at the *back* of a projected image of a three-dimensional object—whether, in other words, they would have some understanding that three-dimensional objects have a number of sides to explore. This was determined by showing images of hollow objects and tracking babies' eye movements to see if they only looked at the front of the object, or if they also looked at the back.

Only some babies figured out three-dimensional objects—the ones reported by parents to have had a lot of experience sitting up (that is, who had more of an ability to explore and manipulate objects). Researchers found that the extent to which babies manipulated objects was associated with their perception of the three-dimensional nature of the images in the other task. The babies who were intrigued by the hollow 3-D objects understood that there was something more to be discovered, and they directed their visual attention to explore that. They were already *trained* to be active explorers.

Taking into account these findings, you can use strategic positioning—supporting the seated and prone positions—to develop your baby's muscles and give him or her a foundation for early sensory and perceptual discovery. As babies develop the capacity to hold and manipulate objects, facilitate their developing motor skills by helping them get to the objects that interest them. As babies find their way to objects, encourage active physical manipulation of the objects. For example, in addition to giving a baby a toy to play with, you can provide fun and stimulating "challenges" for them by placing a toy within reach. If they are sitting, put the toy close enough for them to reach for it; if they are crawling, put it in their general proximity. Position them to do the work of babyhood and you will be encouraging an active exploration of their environment that yields *endless* cognitive benefits.

## Why We Need Children's Museums

We've focused thus far on babies to underscore how essential it is for parents to nurture and reinforce the developmental instinct of exploration. But the role of exploration and discovery does not end after the first year of life. All young children have an aptitude for exploring, manipulating, and discovering, and parents need to embrace and support such inquisitiveness. Jen's father, a science teacher, inspired close observation of the natural world—questioning, exploring, and recording information on their daily outings. And he made every walk down the street or in the backyard an adventure—an opportunity to see something she had never noticed before. A caterpillar underneath a milkweed leaf, a worm under a rock, the way a weed shined silver when run underneath water: These things normally escaped Jen's notice. Instead, thanks to her dad, she learned to live with her radar screen on, always looking to spot something she didn't know was there.

Toddlerhood and early childhood are key developmental periods for ingraining the entrepreneurial spirit of cognitive exploration. In part this is because kids at these ages begin to make more and more choices about how they approach their immediate world. They are also becoming even more receptive to cues they get from parents and other adults about how to approach their environment. Do adults see the world as a place for exploration, manipulation, and discovery? Are their local environments (home, school, nature) exciting places that inspire exploration? Is their psychological environment one that reinforces this perspective and encourages them to take in and understand the world around them in new and exciting ways?

Kate Wells is the chief executive officer of the Children's Museum of Phoenix (CMP), rated by *Parents* magazine as one of the top ten children's museums in the country. Wells is also an entrepreneur of sorts with an emphasis on supporting fundraising ventures. Her experience with the CMP originated when it was in the planning stages; Wells played a prominent role in raising $12.3 million (through a campaign aptly named "Childhood Dreams Built by You") to see the completion of the CMP. Explaining why she directed her energies to organizing the large-scale efforts, Wells cites her experiences as a parent: "My daughter Phoebe pointed out the window one day and said, 'That's the museum my mom built for me' . . . That's why I built it . . . I wanted to create the world my kids grow up in."

What principles went into the design of that world? The overall vision is to "foster a joy of learning." Especially important for toddlers and children are activities where they can touch and manipulate objects. It's worth taking a virtual tour of the Children's Museum of Phoenix, which Kate Wells now oversees as CEO. A young child walking into the CMP will first see a huge, 37-foot-tall structure, the "Schuff-Perini Climber." The structure supports a number of unique appendages, including a bathtub, a boat, a rocket, and a gangplank. Kids are visually invited to explore via steps, sloping walkways, and wooden climbing tunnels. When they get to the top, they are treated to a bird's-eye view of the museum.

But that's just the beginning. Continuing with their visit, kids will encounter a number of exhibits that are also "thoughtfully designed to be unique, to arouse curiosity, and to engage the minds, muscles, and imaginations of our visitors." There is an Art Studio that houses a number of age-appropriate crafting materials (including "gobs of glue") to engage all those fine motor skills so critical to development. Building Big provides a range of raw materials that can be used to build forts and dens, and there is a ladder that provides a perch above the floor. Gross motor skills are promoted in Ian's Corner, which has a number of uniquely shaped "cars" (one is a pickle) that toddlers can drive around by themselves. And the Market is a large space that functions as a pretend café, grocery store, and kitchen. There are real foods kids can manipulate (they can weigh peas, for instance) along with plenty of play materials such as felts and fabrics that can be used to prepare delicacies such as "pizzas" that can be baked in the "ovens." All necessary notes are hit here—encouragement of fine and gross motor skills, opportunities to manipulate in order to discover, and no rules or road maps to follow.

In describing the CMP's facilities, Wells presents them as especially worthwhile given the conditions of childhood today. "Young children do not get enough opportunities to explore without interference or interruption," she explains. "They spend too much time in prescriptive environments where they are told what to do and how to do it. We need to correct that unfortunate trend, giving them space and materials to let their instincts as learners take over as they physically explore their world. It's what they do naturally and unfortunately what is being inhibited with increasing frequency." Wells isn't alone in perceiving the need for more hands-on learning. In February 2014, Brigham Young University's student-produced news website "The Digital Universe" published a story about one of their famous alumni, Tom Dickson, founder of the highly successful Blendtec Company. Dickson was making news because he pledged $2 million to support the construction of the Museum of Natural Curiosity at Thanksgiving Point in Lehi, Utah. The museum will have more than 150 hands-on exhibits, all designed to encourage free-form exploration and experimentation, with an emphasis on physical manipulation. What motivated Dickson to make such a substantial contribution? According to "The Digital Universe," his rationale was the following: "The problem with our society is we do not offer many places for children to enhance existing and develop new desires for learning or to express their creativity."

## Create a Children's Museum at Home

While frequent trips to a children's museum are a great thing to do with your kids, Kate Wells suggests that you can create opportunities for exploration at home by borrowing from specific elements of a children's museum that are simple to recreate. An example from the CMP is the Market, where kids are encouraged to use simple materials to "make" foods to be "cooked." Wells suggests that you don't need to buy "play foods" for children (though those are fine, too); the museum intentionally uses common materials that you will have at home. Cut up fabrics to get different textures and colors. Encourage toddlers to identify different items such as "bacon" and "lettuce." Ask them to make you "salads" and prepare "pizzas." Create an "oven" out of an empty box so they can cook. These are very inexpensive ways to utilize materials around the house to stimulate a toddler. In fact, we'd suggest that the more "imaginary" the materials, the better; kids will be encouraged to think more abstractly as they explore all the ways these common items can be transformed.

If you doubt that ordinary household items will engage your children, take them to a children's museum (there are many fine ones throughout the country) and observe how naturally they take to this type of opportunity. While you are there, stroll around the museum and closely observe the children there. As Wells told us, it's very unusual to see a child who is not engrossed in an activity. You don't see much running around and you don't see much boredom. You see kids in that wonderful "zone" of being completely engaged. It's high-level fun that their brains need.

Limits clearly exist to how far you can turn your home into a children's museum. Not everything at your home—and other people's homes—is to be touched. You do need to say "no" to your children and rein in their exploration at times. But there are ways to do this without denying discovery. Letting your child run wild anytime and anywhere doesn't support discovery. Discovery comes from knowing where and when you can explore and then having the motivation (and, in some sense, the "permission" to do so). Wells puts it this way: "The goal is to reinforce discovery by teaching children when, where, and how to explore. This is a life skill about finding the opportunities for hands-on exploration and manipulation. It's important to know how to pick your spots and what to do with them when you find them." Even in a children's museum, not everything is hands-on (like the gift shop, for instance). The world, even a world designed for children, still has parameters to be respected.

Striking a balance between exploration and boundaries can be somewhat tricky. A successful approach, taught with regularity to parents in parent-training seminars and interventions, is the art of *redirection*, in which you suggest a replacement behavior for the behavior that is not acceptable. Redirection replaces the endless beat of "no no no" with a suggestion that allows for a "yes" response. It tells kids what to do, as opposed to only what *not* to do. For example, while banging on a glass table is a no, the act of banging can be redirected to a pot in a play area. Running over to the oven while you are taking out a steaming chicken is a no; getting a pretend chicken out of a pretend oven is a yes. Redirection turns "no's" into "yesses" in a proactive way that keeps kids safe and teaches boundaries while preserving the exploratory spirit. Too many "no's" inhibit kids' ability to explore. Too many "yesses" doesn't teach them that they have to seek out the *right* opportunities. To get the balance right, Wells suggests that you think of yourself as your child's "playologist."

As a playologist, *you* define play zones and off-limit zones. By encouraging and facilitating exploration in play zones (both practically and psychologically), you will be promoting healthy limit setting without muting the instinct you want to cultivate. For example, you can designate one of your kitchen drawers as an "explore drawer" filled with play materials available to your child. This allows children to understand what's fair game for play and what's off-limits. To encourage pretend cooking, set up their play oven and some type of devoted space for their "ingredients" in a corner of a room that is safe for play (and also not too close to the real oven). Set up a play "garage" where "repairs" can get done or "cars" can be brought in for service. Follow your, and your child's, inner muses.

Of course, as children get older, you can encourage all kinds of exploration with *real* objects and materials. Wells reports that her experiences growing up shaped the perspective she brought to building and running the CMP, specifically the sense of freedom she knew—freedom to explore, experiment, choose, and experience. Her formative experiences did not involve or require special materials or a heavy investment in technology. Mostly, she was involved in chores or other activities that her parents were doing. She remembers being exposed at the grocery store, for example, to all kinds of foods—not just by tasting either, but by taking them in visually and experiencing what they feel like. Noting that parents can borrow this idea, she suggests something she did when her children were young (which they all enjoyed): Take your kids to the grocery store and have them pick out the weirdest-looking fruit they can find. They get a range of sensory experiences: visual and tactile. When you get home, have them participate (as much as possible) as you prepare the fruit. For example, if it needs to be peeled, let them watch and touch. If you cut into the fruit, let them see what it looks like inside. Then, of course, they get to taste what they selected.

You can include, in appropriate ways, your child in your own activities. While there are no big rules here—typically if something interests you, your child will be interested as well—there are some considerations to make the experience optimal. While there are times your children join you in activities such as grocery shopping when you are under a time crunch and feeling rushed or stressed, try to find times to take them to the store to let them experience the freedom of messing around. Don't put pressure on your children to perform tasks that are high stakes for you; it's better if you include them by having them do things that don't carry too much responsibility. Remember, the principle is to find ways for them to get a taste of what you are doing, get their hands a little dirty, and expose their developing minds to the pleasure of exploring all kinds of ways to be engaged. So if you are in a rush, that isn't the time to ask your three-year-old to sort through all the types of apples to help find the one you need for a recipe. Find another time when you can relax and let your kid wander through the produce and begin to wonder why there are so many different types of apples.

## "Don't Yuck My Yum"

Everything we've discussed thus far will help children establish a cognitive basis for exploration and discovery early in life. Another benefit for children who embrace the idea of trying out new things and experiences—who are "open to experience"— is that they get into the habit of finding out, for themselves, what they do and don't like. This is a powerful thing to discover when you are young. You begin to realize that you gravitate to some things rather than others, and experience teaches you what you want to pursue with greater depth.

But there's a caveat here, and an opportunity for parents to provide some guidance and nuance that will further cultivate their child's openness to experience. "Likes" and "dislikes" should be shaped as personal preferences rather than dogmatic conclusions. Children do need to learn to respect other people's choices, gained via their own exploration and discovery. They must learn that the world offers opportunities for all kinds of discoveries, each of which is to be valued. If we don't emphasize the personal nature of preference, kids can lean toward becoming closed-minded, negating the essence of cognitive exploration. Children's Museum of Phoenix CEO Kate Wells has a unique way of expressing this: "In our family we like to say, 'Don't yuck my yum!' In other words, if I like something, and you don't, respect my choice to like it. Similarly, I'll respect your choice to like what you like."

As a parent, you can encourage tolerance in many ways. Here are just a few ideas for how to practice this principle. When it comes to food preferences, acknowledge what your child likes and doesn't like—but remind them that other people might like what they don't. Encourage your kids to keep trying some foods they aren't that fond of. Even if they never like it, you are cultivating the idea of continued exploration and openness to contrary ideas and instilling the notion that at some point they might eventually change their mind. The same thinking applies to other domains as well. Display enthusiasm for kids' emerging interests (for example, playing with cars and trucks, making artwork, riding a bike) but convey equal value to other activities that they decide they don't want to pursue. To this point, encourage children to try, now and again, activities that aren't their favorites. For example, if they aren't too keen on going down a slide and prefer less physical activities, expose them to the playground anyway and encourage them to think about trying it occasionally.

Openness to experience offers inherent rewards that persist through every phase of our lives. Openness also lays the foundation for children to pursue their potential to the fullest. Kids are "wired" for discovery, but we as parents have it in our power to help them explore the world with energy and enthusiasm. A few well-placed words or actions can make a world of difference.

## The Academic "Edge"

At this point, you may not have trouble agreeing that these organic, everyday moments—talking to a baby, encouraging a baby to reach for toys, giving toddlers opportunities for free play, setting up areas in your home for your toddler to play with simple materials—are good ways to parent. Perhaps you will retract a little bit from the idea that technology, in the first few years of life, is not established as a fundamentally important way to develop the brain (again, we really don't know much at this point in terms of the research), but we suspect that it's hard to argue with the idea that babies and toddlers are primed to explore, and that parents can nurture this instinct.

The real parenting challenge comes when children get older. We've alluded to some of the pressures in the modern world of parenting, particularly as children begin schooling. We've referenced troubling trends, like cutting back recess time in kindergarten and beyond, that reflect the misplaced perception that we need to more strongly emphasize academic pursuits. Given that developmental researchers, pediatricians, and educators have long championed the importance of hands-on exploration and discovery, why are some toddlers and young children not getting sufficient opportunity to develop these skills in preschool and child care? Why would the commitment to fostering the physical and cognitive components of pure exploration and discovery be slipping when we place our children in the hands of trained professionals?

We can speculate that it's all about the drive to make sure our kids are as competitive as possible, as early as possible. And it's not hard to see why parents feel this pressure. There are waiting lists for many preschools. Lotteries may determine which school a child attends. It's not uncommon to begin to talk about college preparation in kindergarten (recall the example of eliminating a school play to ensure maximal effort devoted to academic training). A climate of testing and evaluating young children can permeate parental perspectives, and it's natural for parents to want to do everything they can to help their child get an edge as early as possible. And schools feel the pressure, too—they ultimately have to, in some sense, serve parents.

This collective preoccupation with laying the foundations for academic success early in life creates a vortex in which both parents and educators can stray from what we've learned from decades of research on childhood. In a study published in *Pediatrics*, nine focus groups comprised of child care teachers and providers offered perceptions about "facilitators and barriers" to children's playtime. Researchers found that *parents* were increasingly concerned about what their kids were "learning," fearing that too much playtime would impede academic progress. The majority of parents surveyed were not interested in gross and fine motor development; as a result, teachers and providers felt palpable pressure to emphasize traditional academics and decrease time devoted to play. Consider a concluding message offered by the authors of the paper: "Recognizing that school readiness is a prevalent concern, pediatricians may need to highlight for parents the many learning benefits of outdoor play (better concentration, learning about science, negotiation with peers) and reassure parents that active time does not need to come at the expense of time dedicated to 'academics' and 'learning.'"

We might think that preschools give toddlers an edge by bypassing recess for accelerated mathematical and linguistic fluency. But the truth is that preschoolers *need* to play. They need to climb to the top of the jungle gym and chase their friends around the soccer field. They need to paint with watercolors and build tall towers with blocks. They need to explore their world. If we fail to accommodate this need, we might end up with rooms full of kids squirming around, seemingly unable to pay attention when in fact they are simply not being engaged properly. Some experts are even worried that some toddlers may even be diagnosed incorrectly with ADHD in highly (and inappropriately) structured classrooms.

It's ironic that while we're busy turning preschools into workplaces, actual workplaces are increasingly embracing the idea of having playtime and play areas. "Playful workplaces" are springing up in top companies around the world. The toy manufacturer LEGO, the social games developer Zynga, and

Google all offer specific areas designated for play in the office. Many advertising agencies have Ping-Pong, foosball, and video games on hand to help stimulate creativity. Managers in corporate environments are sensing that free movement, thought, and interaction with others lead to better ideas and productivity.

With kids, we continue to see scientific evidence that fine motor development cultivated by play correlates with academic readiness and achievement. As one study demonstrated, the simple act of learning to copy basic shapes at ages two and three predicted academic performance in kindergarten, even after accounting for a host of factors. This is because kids with good fine motor skills don't have to expend cognitive energy holding their writing instruments; instead, they can focus on learning how to write and process letters and words and numbers.

This is what we mean by "academic readiness"—a familiar concept we believe is well worth embracing. The first seven years of life are designed to help kids develop all the skills they will need to pursue their academic studies well—they aren't the years for *mastering* those skills. Think about reading. Reading to toddlers is one of the best things you can do for your child. But the goal isn't to use it as a means of inducing prodigal reading skills. In fact, evidence suggests that toddlers will get more out of being read to if you treat it as *play*. For example, toddlers who are encouraged to act out a story as they are listening to it have been shown to understand the story better. The traditional notion that a toddler needs to "sit still" in order to listen while you read to them is at odds with the idea that they need to bring all of their skills to discover how to explore a story.

## Homework Overload

The dangers of providing too much academic structure is also borne out on research regarding homework. Kids in kindergarten may get homework these days; kids in fourth grade may have *two hours* of homework a night. As developmental researchers converge on the idea that childhood should be filled with opportunities for physical and cognitive exploration, homework appears as yet another competing element that can trump the time available for those pursuits.

A white paper offered by the research organization Challenge Success, housed at the Stanford Graduate School of Education, suggests that we need to take a good look at the homework demands we place on children of all ages. Let's start with the youngest group: elementary school children. Research suggests that there is essentially *no* correlation between time spent completing homework in these grades and academic achievement. Thus, the idea of a fourth grader having two hours of homework at night needs to be revisited—to say the least.

How about middle school? Here there is some statistical association between homework and grades, but it maxes out when nightly homework exceeds sixty to ninety minutes. The principle for this age bracket is: Less is more. A similar principle holds for high school students: Exceeding two hours a night leads to diminishing returns in terms of student achievement. Excessive homework often involves repetitive activities that diminish student engagement—so while less is more, homework should also be truly productive and not just added drudgery. Any unnecessary time spent on homework can impact children's sleep and especially their opportunities for free time and activities of their choosing. Thinking back to the sense of wonder a baby brings to studying the human face, how does repetitive and even counterproductive activity foster cognitive exploration and a desire to search out new ideas and information?

So what's a parent to do? Parents can't dictate school policy. But as we've seen, they have a voice that is heard by educators. Parents should keep on eye on the amount of homework kids are receiving and have productive conversations with the school's administration to make sure that homework isn't defeating its intended purpose. Parents can take stock of the research and consider the idea that many people who achieve substantial success—particularly entrepreneurs—believe in the importance of cultivating exploration and, in fact, are crafting work environments that are designed to promote play in the cognitive sense of the word. In addition to asking a preschool to describe their curriculum for reading and mathematics, inquire about the opportunities for exploration in the classroom and outside. Find out if a school is cutting recess time and make the case that this is not warranted. Keep an eye on your child to see if they are developing a love of learning, and a sense of exploration that is reinforced in school. For some parents, a hard choice may present itself—perhaps you will decide that you don't want your child to attend a school that emphasizes giving your child an academic edge when, in fact, it is reducing many of the elements that lay the foundation for just that. It can be the most slippery slope for a parent, given the emotional nature of the issue and the very real pressures to make sure your child is getting the best experiences early in life. But as we've seen, the key here is to make sure that your child is equipped to know how to explore and is open to a wide range of experiences. That's as important as learning academic subject matter and, in fact, supports not only scholastic progress, but the real pathways to eventual personal successes.

# 2

||||||||||||||||||||

# PRIMED TO INNOVATE

In 2012, the American Public Media show *Marketplace* commissioned a survey of more than 700 employers to find out what skills or talents they sought in college graduates. The results were unsettling. Employers expressed concern that graduates lacked the skills deemed most essential in the workplace, such as the "ability to solve complex problems." It wasn't that recent graduates weren't well educated or proficient; rather, the considerable knowledge base they possessed was not a core skill needed in the "real world." According to respondents, it was far more important that graduates demonstrate an ability to make sense of large and sometimes disparate bodies of information and be able to approach complicated issues in new and better ways.

Dr. Tony Wagner, expert in residence at Harvard University's

Innovation Lab and author of the influential book *Creating Innovators: The Making of Young People Who Will Change the World*, elaborated on these findings in an interview with us. He suggested that the fundamental skills that will position youth for success "no longer center on knowledge acquisition, but rather knowledge application." The kind of knowledge you acquire by mastering facts and demonstrating proficiency on tests is just not a special talent anymore. Knowledge is everywhere, easily accessible by a simple mouse click. The primary ability children will need going forward, Dr. Wagner asserts, is the ability to *innovate*. With markets more competitive and complex than ever, workers today face tougher, more insistent problems on the job. Career success will come by "not just having knowledge but doing something with knowledge to solve problems."

Innovation isn't just for entrepreneurs who will create new technologies, businesses, or practices. *All* of us must become strong innovators, Wagner believes, and that holds no matter what your field or job may be. The youth who will stand out in the employment marketplace will be those whose skill sets support innovative thinking—and not necessarily those who excel academically. Wagner references Google's recent shift in hiring practices as a prime example. In an interview with Thomas L. Friedman of the *New York Times*, Laszlo Bock, Google's senior vice president of people operations, stated that "learning ability" is the trait that Google now looks for. "It's the ability to process on the fly," Laszlo explained. "It's the ability to pull together disparate bits of information." Google gets the future. They want to hire entrepreneurial types who don't merely explore their changing world but also *create* in it. And while we aren't saying that many fields don't require "knowledge," bear in mind how rapidly that knowledge changes. Anytime you go to a doctor, you want to know that that doctor not only assimilates all the latest findings and implications for clinical practice, but is also highly skilled in working through the fuzziness that characterizes the imprecise art of differential diagnosis.

It can be argued that our current educational climate does not encourage the entrepreneur's style of innovative thinking. Zealous efforts to standardize learning and assessment—and the resulting habit of "teaching to the test"—pull children away from their natural affinity toward innovation. A nonstop emphasis on mastering material rather than thinking "outside of the box" may lead to high grades and test scores, but it doesn't necessarily breed the kind of cognitive dexterity that Wagner describes. And Wagner is not alone. Po Bronson and Ashley Merryman, authors of the influential book *NurtureShock: New Thinking About Children*, wrote an article called "The Creativity Crisis," describing recent evidence that our current generation of youth is scoring lower than prior generations on standardized measures of creativity—a trend they suggest that has been growing since 1990. In his hugely influential TED talk titled "How Schools Kill Creativity," Sir Kenneth Robinson argued that all children have the capacity for creativity but our educational systems do not properly cultivate it and, in fact, actively *discourage* creativity and innovative thinking. Our schools emphasize at earlier and earlier ages that there is *one "right" answer* or way to do something. This practice directly undermines one of the core aspects of innovation, which is to embrace multiple approaches to a problem in order to find a solution.

Let's imagine the experience of young students today. Think about all the critiques they may hear when they are doing something as simple as coloring. They may be told to "stay in the lines" and that there is no such thing as blue dogs or green skies or orange grass. Similar restrictions may apply in their early academic experiences as well. They may learn that mathematical problems have one—and only one—answer and way to find it. If children challenge, or even question, a scientific "fact," they are told they are wrong and are penalized with red ink. The message delivered in these scenarios is that any attempt to innovate—to think of something new or original—is, in essence, equated with failure.

While we are not suggesting that there is no utility to absorbing "facts," the stark reality is that a strict adherence to making children focus on digesting and mastering information undermines their inherent abilities to innovate and results in an outdated skill set. You cannot innovate if you are inhibited from challenging the known and the accepted, and if you are conditioned to worry about avoiding being "wrong." As a researcher, Richard has always been fond of the saying that "one person's error term is another person's dissertation." The point is that researchers, just like any innovator, have to start with challenging what we think we know, take on the messy or unknown, and push ahead, not being intimidated by testing out new ideas that might not necessarily pan out. Children are actually very well equipped—cognitively and emotionally—to do these things, and parents and educators can capitalize on this by fostering more opportunities to cultivate innovation.

## Insights on Innovation from the Workplace

When we think of creativity, we tend to focus on the arts, and perhaps the sciences. We think of big achievements. Game changers. Pioneers or mavericks whose success reaches a level most don't achieve in life. We think of Picasso and Einstein, Beethoven and the Beatles. Innovation, by contrast, is more accessible and arguably more relevant on a daily basis. Echoing the voices of Ted Robinson and Tony Wagner, *innovative thinking*—the ability to come up with new solutions and approaches to existing problems—can and should permeate the everyday experiences of adults as well as children. We all can potentially discover novel ways of attracting new customers, or tackling an algebra equation, or performing household chores. Such core "thinking" skills are actually possessed by all children, and they can be further developed through proper encouragement and nurturing. And this is where the life experiences and insights of entrepreneurial thinkers from multiple fields can help us understand how innovation is defined and championed day to day in the workplace.

Ohio-based Elmer's Products Inc. has played a role in nearly every American childhood. Most parents remember using Elmer's Glue at home to make crafts and in school to create projects. Elmer's remains a leader in the adhesives and crafting markets, and the company strongly supports activities that enhance the development of innovation in childhood. Elmer's also cultivates innovative thinking in their own workplace, and even offers an open portal for people outside the company to submit ideas to them.

Dana Conover is Elmer's director of innovation and new products. In an interview with us, he echoes Tony Wagner in pinpointing the challenge facing recent graduates and younger employees: "The old paradigms don't work for them anymore. Information is ubiquitous, and anyone can get 'knowledge' and 'facts' pretty easily." So what, then, would a company like Elmer's prize in their younger employees? "Critical thinking skills are paramount. You need to be able to think on your own, and use every resource and every tool at your disposal. You have to develop and apply the ability to analyze and dissect issues, and consider every possible angle to gaining traction on a problem. And of course you need to be able to act on this." Conover not only deeply believes that all individuals can *learn* these skills, but also puts this idea into practice in the workplace via Elmer's practices to cultivate innovative thinking throughout its workforce on a daily basis.

Conover's colleague Joe Wetli, Elmer's director of innovation and new business development, offers the idea that innovative thinking involves finding "unique ways of looking at problems. A key is 'contextual thinking'—a way of seeing the big picture to understand the situation at hand and consider different paths to get to a solution rather than using the prescribed methods that are easily available." Similarly, Jen subscribes to the idea that everyone at her firm can practice "daily innovation." She is particularly pleased when someone simply suggests a procedural tweak or new way of getting things done, along the lines of "Why are we doing this like this, and not like that?" It's those small sparks that often set the stage for the bigger changes in practice that lead to offering a novel solution to a client, identifying a new customer need, or generating a breakthrough approach to a challenging project.

"Daily innovation" isn't limited to the workplace, or to adults. Given the opportunity, children take naturally to innovative thinking—the practice of looking at something with a fresh eye, merging different perspectives, and seeing new dots that can be connected in order to make something better. This doesn't require specialized training, fads, or lots of money, as opportunities for "daily innovation" arise—for both adults and kids—in the flow of everyday life.

## A Young Innovator's Story

Entrepreneur Rachel Brooks, cofounder of the e-commerce company Citizen Made, doesn't just subscribe to these ideas; she's lived them. Only in her midtwenties, Brooks has already received recognition as an innovator, including being named one of Women Innovate Mobile's Female Founders to Watch, and Dell's #Inspire 100 list in 2012. What achievement got Dell's attention? As explained in their press release, the #Inspire 100 list singles out "thinkers, designers, and risk takers" who are "moved by their individual passions and who inspire others to do the same." The explicit focus was on influencers who have used technology to empower and inspire others.

Brooks has done exactly that. The endpoint of her business Citizen Made is to use technology to spur more creative and collaborative fashion designing by allowing retailers to customize their products *with* their customers. A company that makes T-shirts can use Citizen Made to interact with customers who want to include something unique in the design of their shirt. This cocreation can happen in real time via the Citizen Made website and can be used by companies of any size anywhere in the world, thanks to software developed by Brooks and cofounder Bryn McCoy. Using technology to connect retailers to customers and facilitate collaboration in tailoring products is nothing short of a game changer in the design world. Brooks's technological innovation was fueled not only by her skills in software design, but also by merging a number of interests across a variety of disciplines.

Although she had a long-standing interest in the arts, Brooks focused on business in college, attending University of Michigan's Stephen M. Ross School of Business. She told us that although she did well academically, she made a conscious decision *not* to focus all her energies on attaining high grades. Brooks valued the importance of taking a variety of classes that interested her—even if she wasn't sure she could get an A in them. So she did not dispense with her "conflicting" interest in the arts even though she was concentrating on business. This lay a foundation for Brooks to weave together her many interests after graduation. She cultivated an interest in fashion while working at a prominent department store in New York. Then, she worked at a large Chicago-based advertising agency, where she learned about digital products and *taught herself* computer programming. Combining art, business, advertising, and digital expertise, she went on to create Citizen Made—a win-win situation for customers and sellers alike.

Brooks described to us childhood experiences that contributed to her embrace of innovation. She recalls always having a never-ending curiosity, loving the idea of learning and exploring for its own sake. In her experience, those early elements of discovery evolved into the rudiments of innovation. She breaks the evolution down into three questions she has found herself asking since childhood: "How can I explore this further? What is attracting my interest? How can I make it better?"

## "Make It Better"

*The "make it better" part is the essence of the process of innovation.* Today Brooks understands that, as a child, she cultivated an internal drive to use opportunities for exploration as a platform to discover how to dig deeper into the areas that interested her. She remembers always wanting to understand something well enough to do something new with it. Her childhood was not jam-packed with structured activities or the pressure to excel in one specific area. Rather, there was "a lot of doing going on in the house without a big endpoint." Her mom was an active seamstress who crafted clothes for Brooks on a regular basis. As a child, Brooks understood that her mom had "the power to create something," that she could go from the idea to the design to, finally, the execution. Over the years, Brooks learned the craft of sewing, and true to the Citizen Made's spirit, she makes her own clothes now—including many of the outfits she wears to business meetings and pitches.

Just as important, Brooks's parents encouraged a number of other artistic activities that served to cultivate her curiosity and foster her innovative thinking. Drawing and painting dominated Brooks's childhood, and music was important, too. For the most part, these were things the Brooks kids did on their own, without much concern about the outcome (that is, whether they were, or would become, "good"). The one structured activity imposed on Brooks was piano lessons, which she took every week for thirteen years. Interestingly, this is the one childhood activity she remembers not looking forward to—"In fact, I hated it!"

The overall message of these trips and her childhood as a whole, Brooks remembers, was to "find and follow your passions" rather than "being pushed into high achievement." It's what Harvard's Tony Wagner refers to as the triad of "play, passion, purpose." Early opportunities for play help children find their passions, which lead to an eventual purpose fueled by their own drive. Brooks developed an emerging sense of self-direction and purpose, and a drive to understand not only how things worked, but how she could make things work better. This is what the entrepreneurial thinker is so good at. And like entrepreneurs, all kids have this capacity, but it needs to be nourished and supported rather than squelched.

## Exposure + Talk + Opportunity = Innovation Seekers

Is there no value to signing up for structured activities so children can get "good" at something at a young age? There is, but parents should keep three principles in mind. First, devoting *too much time* to structured activities can deprive children of the benefits gained during *unstructured* time. Part of an innovative approach to *anything* involves bringing a variety of perspectives to an issue. Exposure to music, sports, technology, cooking—the list could go on and on—gives young minds a chance to sample different fields and engage in different types of thinking. And there is no substitute for encouraging a child to try different things throughout the formative years. So even if your five-year-old seems like a budding dancer, athlete, computer programmer—whatever—leave some time for other activities that can be done around the house, and encourage some sampling. You can continue this practice throughout childhood, adolescence, and the teen years.

Second, when a child is engaged in a structured activity, the focus is typically on learning that skill. Again, that's not a bad thing and, in fact, is a good thing. But think back to the many things Rachel Brooks absorbed when doing things with her parents out in the world. Knowledge of various kinds is as important as specific skills, and for that you often need unstructured activities. As a parent, you can infuse valuable learning into your kids' daily routine. Have a favorite restaurant? Share with your child why you think that establishment stands out above all the other options. Admire a sports star? What unique things does that athlete do that stand out? Childhood isn't just a time to develop skills that come from training and practice—it's also a period when life lessons regarding innovation can be absorbed. Your child may gain far more at age five by becoming attuned to what makes a restaurant excellent than he does by mastering cooking skills.

Third, structured activities don't always allow kids to discover their own interests. In a strategic yet open-ended approach, kids can nurture passions that in turn allow innovative skills to flourish. Your child's inherent curiosity will lead them to wonder how to figure things out, solve a problem, and put ideas together in new ways. What could be better than that?

Like the Brooks family's climate, the one Jen knew growing up also encouraged an appreciation of the many types of cognitive stimulation in the world. There were no mandates about the *areas* that should be investigated; rather, Jen absorbed a more abstract idea that whatever excites you can be pursued in more depth. As a result, Jen was inclined and empowered to find her inner entrepreneur at an early age. She would spend hours creating board games, inventing the concept, designing the board and its pieces, and creating the box and packaging. Her most prized board game creation was called Fashion Fads. Each participant received a boy or a girl character with a different fashion obsession. Characters had to move around the board and acquire different pieces of an outfit to make their trendy ensemble complete. Fashion Fads took Jen months to complete, and afterward, she enjoyed playing it with her friends.

It's interesting to consider the similarities and differences between Jen and her brother, James. James also gravitated toward innovation, but in a very different way. From a young age he was obsessed with fishing, and he also had a budding interest in art and writing. During the family's cross-country travels, he would catch different types of trout, paint them, and write about his travels in a journal. He pursued this passion through adolescence, and in his freshman year of college was encouraged by a journalist friend to send his work to a publisher. An outdoorsman and editor at Alfred Knopf recognized the uniqueness of his work and published him. He was nineteen years old, and his book of paintings and writings about the trout of North America sold more than 100,000 copies—helping fuel the fly-fishing mania that swept the nation at the time. In the Prosek family, two siblings with different interests had one big thing in common: They grew up learning to pursue passions and innovate boldly.

# "Counterfactual Thinking":
## The Sophistication of the Young Mind

Developmental researchers have begun to uncover some of the specific ways in which young children demonstrate their emerging tendencies toward innovative thinking. This growing area of research is providing insight into the somewhat surprising ways to best encourage the growth of these sophisticated young minds—and yields simple strategies that can help parents foster innovation in their children.

Let's start with pretend play, which has frequently been cited as a primary way children develop creativity. As children, we all had imaginary friends, fought wars using toy soldiers, or imagined we were princesses going to the royal ball. For decades, scientists have viewed such pretend play (that is, pretending an object is something it isn't, or pretending to be someone you aren't) as a core influence on creativity in the early years. And that makes sense: Isn't pretending to be someone else one of the most creative things a young child can do?

The question, though, is what is the young mind doing when engaged in pretend—because, as developmental psychologist Angeline Lillard has proposed, pretend is hardly the only way that kids can engage in creative thinking. As we probe deeper into the literature, we are able to isolate elements that make *many types of activity* in the early years productive and stimulating with respect to innovation. The concepts can get a bit heady, but they have strong implications for parenting and child development. Drs. Caren Walker and Alison Gopnik suggest that pretend—or more specifically "pretense"—is a way children develop "counterfactual reasoning," or the ability to consider possible alternatives to something that has already happened. It's also a way of figuring out possibilities for the future based on observations of the past. Counterfactual reasoning strongly supports the development of innovative thinking because it is a powerful and natural way for children to think about "what if" based on "what was"—and also "what could be." This capacity can be either reinforced or squashed by adults, leading to the concern noted earlier that our culture is not giving kids enough opportunities to practice innovative thinking.

It's actually very easy to encourage your child to use pretend in multiple ways. An especially important developmental period for encouraging this kind of cognitive activity is the preschool years—an age when we often see children gravitate instinctively to pretend. For example, it's fun for a toddler to pretend that two cars are racing. It would be interesting to them to see what happens if they crash into each other. But you could further stimulate counterfactual reasoning if you asked what would happen if one car started going slower than the other car, or if one swerved in the opposite direction. Your toddler would have to think through the various possibilities, derived in part from what they have already observed, but driven by generating scenarios that they haven't seen yet.

It's also important to become an *observer* of your child, and recognize when they are spontaneously practicing counterfactual reasoning so you don't inadvertently discourage it. Take the car racing example. Maybe you spend time setting up a racetrack, and then your child focuses on creating crashes or making the cars fly off the track. Your instinct might be to think that they aren't using the cars "properly." You might even intervene to help keep the cars on the track. A more productive strategy would be to become a play partner who is interested in what's happening when the cars collide or crash. This gives you an opportunity to watch your child's sophisticated counterfactual reasoning skills come to life.

## Less Is More: Guiding Versus Teaching

We can identify two key principles for encouraging counterfactual reasoning: Let your child lead the way, and ask questions rather than provide answers or critiques. Keep in mind that critiquing very young children during play—telling them what to do, or directly instructing them—undermines their cognitive development because you, rather than your child, are doing the counterfactual reasoning.

An experiment performed by researcher Laura Schulz and colleagues at MIT elegantly demonstrates this principle. The researchers brought four-year-olds into a laboratory one by one. Each child was shown a new toy—one that had four tubes attached to it. Each tube had some type of special property. One tube made noise if you pulled on it. Another had a mirror in it. The children were assigned to one of two groups. Children in one group watched as the experimenter explained how the toy worked; she deliberately made the toy squeak by pulling on one of the tubes. Then, she left the room to let the toddlers play with the toy. For the second group, the experimenter pulled on the tube as if by accident, and acted surprised when it squeaked—and then said she wanted to try it again to see what would happen. She also left the toddlers in this group alone with the toy.

Alone, children in both groups tried to make the squeaking sound by pulling on the correct tube. But the kids who observed the "accidental" discovery of the squeaky tube *played more* with the other tubes and spent more time exploring. It appeared they were more curious to see if the other tubes did something interesting when a *discovery* was modeled for them, as opposed to receiving direct instruction.

Dr. Alison Gopnik and colleagues carried out a similar experiment with four-year-olds that yielded nearly identical results. Researchers presented two groups of toddlers with a toy that could play music, but only if a series of actions were performed in a particular sequence. One group received direct instruction on these sequences, some of which worked and some of which didn't. The second group watched as the experimenter simply tried out sequences, indicating that she didn't know how it worked. Each of the sequences involved three actions (for example, pull on this, press that, hit this button), but the music only played if the sequence ended with two specific actions. The children in the direct instruction group imitated the experimenter exactly, following the three-action sequence. In contrast, the other group tended to figure out that only two actions were required. They modeled the exploration demonstrated and, in the process, discovered a simpler way of getting the toy to play music (and figured out how it really worked!).

As these studies suggest, kids learn vital skills when they figure things out for themselves. You might think it would be *helpful* to show "proper use" for a particular toy, but, in fact, we are seeing evidence that direct instruction doesn't teach nearly as well as encouraging kids to do their own exploration, manipulation, questioning, probing, and problem solving.

Want additional evidence that less is more? A study published in *Parenting: Science and Practice* videotaped a mom and child while they were playing (they were given different toys by the experimenters). Each pair was observed across a four-year span—from ages one to five. The research team reviewed the videotaped interactions and coded the moms' "directiveness"— the use of commands, requests, or simply telling a kid what to do. They also examined how the kids *reacted* to directives, both in terms of how positively they engaged when playing with Mom and how much negative behavior they displayed.

The results of this study were clear. More directives led to less engaged play over time, and more negative behavior. Maternal negativity (facial expression, tone of voice) also *inhibited* play and elicited "acting out" behavior. The more optimal strategy was to let children take the lead and follow their imagination; *building* on what they do proved to be the most supportive action. Try to resist the temptation to tell your child that there is a "right" way to play with a toy or where their stories "should" go. Replace "How about doing this?" with reinforcing what they are saying. Of course, if they need help or they're doing something dangerous, step in. But, in general, it's best to let kids be in charge of their own play—and commit your-self to playing the role of the willing and curious participant.

**Let kids be in charge of their own play.**

In many ways, using the "less is more" principle at home is similar to what many successful business leaders do in the work-place. Jen has learned that there are diminishing returns to a leader always having to add value—their own "special sauce"— to everyone's activities. This can diminish the enthusiasm and confidence of people when, in principle, their work is often "good enough" and doesn't require direction and enhancement; in fact, this type of interference can inhibit individuals from striving to be innovative, taking away what motivates them to achieve excellence—namely, the joy of discovery and the sat-isfaction of finding solutions that make a meaningful contribu-tion. There are, of course, times when input and oversight are essential—but Jen suggests that the key is to guide rather than teach so that her staff members can feel in their gut the bril-liance of their own work. The same holds true for our kids.

## Taking Things Apart
## (or Deconstructing the World)

Part of understanding comes from taking things apart. Children have a natural tendency to want to deconstruct something to see what's inside, what's connected to what, and how to put things back together again. Richard has heard many stories from parents who recognize this ability—and its importance—in their young children. In one case, a five-year-old boy was having trouble adjusting to kindergarten and specifically to the reading readiness activities in the classroom. The parents began to see this at home as well. Whenever they tried to do reading exercises at home, their son would shut down and want to go "play with his radio" in his room. The parents thought this was an avoidance ploy and would not permit it. Over the course of a week or two, they had a change of heart. Figuring that maybe playing with the radio could be a good thing for their son, they agreed that he could go do so after he finished his reading exercises.

This approach worked, as the boy was much more compliant and his classroom performance noticeably improved. But the parents were somewhat mystified, because when they went past his room, they never heard music playing. One night, they peeked in and saw multiple radio components spread out on the floor. They expressed a bit of dismay that their son was breaking the radio and wondered if he was angry about having to do the reading. He told them he was having fun—he liked to take the radio apart and see how fast he could put it back together again. He began to demonstrate this for them. Twenty years later, he was on his way to establishing a very successful career as an engineer.

Taking things apart is not purposeless—it's a formative, foundational instinct. Being able to deconstruct and reconstruct is powerful for young minds because it is not just an abstract experience, but a real, hands-on adventure. It can be a wonderful surprise to see what kids will do, at their own initiative, with their toys and everyday objects—if they are permitted to do so. The next time you see your child doing something "strange" with a toy, try to get into his or her head and see if you can discern counterfactual thinking in action.

You should also sensitize yourself to what your kids do when faced with a problem—say, a toy that's not working. Or more to the point, you should become more alert to what your child sees *you* doing when faced with this situation. Modeling counterfactual reasoning—engaging in talking about how that toy should work, what might not be working, what you might try to fix it, how you would know if you've solved the problem—encourages your child to reason counterfactually as well. If you seem frustrated by a

> If you seem frustrated by a problem, your child will also start to behave that way.

problem, your child will also start to behave that way. Treating the problem as an opportunity to investigate, learn, and solve makes it more likely that they will use a similar strategy in their own lives.

These opportunities don't arise only when something is broken—they happen every day, whenever your child is trying to do something challenging. Think about how you would interact with your child if you were sitting together and doing a jigsaw puzzle that was somewhat difficult for her. Would you find the pieces for her? Deliver a verbal primer on the guiding principles of how to apply a strategy? Criticize your child when she put two pieces together that don't fit? Or would you model your own inquisitiveness, let your child figure it out on her own, watch her joy when she finds a match, encourage her to keep searching, and model a few successes? All of your actions and words will be amplified 1,000 times—you are setting the tone and manner as the ultimate role model.

## The Arts and Innovation

Many experts have debated over the years whether the arts play a vital role in cultivating innovative thinking throughout childhood. New frameworks now exist that speak specifically to the arts' *cognitive* importance. Jennifer Groff, cofounder of the Centre for Curriculum Redesign and vice president of learning and program development at the Learning Games Network, wrote an influential article in the *Harvard Educational Review* titled "Expanding Our 'Frames' of Mind for Education and the

Arts." She suggests that in the past, we thought that the arts could provide secondary support for other "intelligences" such as mathematics. Groff contends that this framework does not accurately capture how the brain works or how cognitive development unfolds. She proposes instead the concept of "whole-mindedness" in which brain function operates in real time to do two things: process information across multiple senses, and form parallel cognitive representations in order to promote interdisciplinary thinking. Groff proposes that the visual arts should be seen as a *primary* area of education, one that promotes whole-mindedness as a fundamentally important goal of cognitive development.

Dr. Robert Root-Bernstein has led the way in exploring the arts and sciences' function as a catalyst for innovative thinking. A professor of physiology at Michigan State University, he has written extensively with his wife, Dr. Michele Root-Bernstein, on how critically important childhood exposure to the arts is for cultivating innovative thinking in the sciences. Here's one glimpse into the types of insights offered in their writings: "Einstein was certainly not a standout in his mathematics and physics classes. . . . So what were his special talents? One was clearly an ability to visualize concepts in his mind, a talent that was fostered by Aaugau Cantonai School in Switzerland, where he completed his secondary education. . . . One outcome of this training was Einstein's habit of imagining himself riding a light beam or falling in an elevator at the speed of light, the basis of thought experiments that yielded his revolutionary insights."

Stories about Einstein certainly offer tantalizing insight into the importance of innovative thinking and how assessment of "pure" abilities may not provide the most insight into who will be innovative. But, of course, we could wonder how well the principles learned from an Einstein translate to the majority of people. Was he an anomaly who had a unique mind that allowed him to make connections that eluded others? Or is there a more general principle at play that fuels the development and achievement of scientists?

Let's home in on one aspect of the Einstein story: the "thought experiments" that involved visualization. Groff considers learning to perceive three-dimensional objects in childhood as one of the early benefits of the arts. Opportunities to manipulate three-dimensional structures promote higher-order cognitive processes such as spatial rotation—processes that become important when children learn, later in life, subjects such as geometry and chemistry. But the skills go beyond specific content areas. Individuals in many professional arenas try to "visualize" solutions to problems.

Dr. Juan Ivaldi, a highly successful and influential chemist and innovator, agrees. Ivaldi has been a leader in analytic chemistry, merging academic advances in research with innovative product development (he is a coholder of multiple patents in the physical sciences). He described to us how his innovative moments frequently involve visualization: "Innovation is when one sees something others do not see. By 'seeing,' I am talking about a completely abstract, visual concept in the mind. In other words, by not taking things at face value and keeping the mind open to possibilities, opportunities appear . . . There is a confidence and an audacity that goes along with innovation. One must first believe that one has the power to innovate. Then by keenly observing and not taking things for granted, solutions start to appear in the mind. At least, that is how it works for me."

Ivaldi suggests that his innovative breakthroughs happen during contemplation: "There was often a struggle of some kind, for example, a need to understand and improve the performance of a device. In the process of struggling with the problem and taking time to quietly look over the data, innovative thoughts would come to my mind. It was in those quiet moments that a mental model of what was going on would form in my head. Once the model was in place, I could solve the problem."

This process of visualization that scientists practice represents one way in which cognitive processes elicited by the arts and the sciences overlap. According to Ivaldi: "The visual arts are extremely important in terms of cultivating abstract mental visualization. One needs to imagine what could be, based on a model of the observed. . . . [T]he visual arts, which explore dimensions, colors, and shapes, train the mind and give it experience which later becomes the foundation of imagination of how the physical world works. Ultimately, being able to model the complex in one's head leads to a conception in which the explanations of what is going on get reduced to simpler and more basic descriptions. I think of it as looking beneath the surface. And that insight is the essence of how we come to innovative thinking and solutions."

Research conducted by Root-Bernstein with colleagues at

Michigan State University provides new evidence supporting this premise. The researchers studied a number of engineers, honors graduates in STEM (science, technology, engineering, math), and STEM engineers, collecting data on their current involvement with the arts as well as objective indicators of their career achievements. A number of notable findings emerged applying to the group as a whole. For example, honors graduates in STEM are three to ten times more likely to be involved in the arts as compared to national norms. Perhaps more telling, the research team also looked at what they called "creative capital"—the extent to which individuals in the study filed copyrights, filed and licensed patents, established companies, and published papers and/or books. The tendency to produce creative capital was highly associated with a "sustained" involvement (meaning it was a regular feature in their life) with the arts.

You might wonder if something else was driving these findings, such as money. Maybe involvement in the arts simply reflected economic advantage—families with extensive financial resources may have been better positioned to facilitate their children's involvement in the arts. This was not the case; the research team determined that family wealth was *not* predictive of childhood exposure to the arts, or the creative capital measures. What did matter was just *participating* in the arts in early childhood and *sustaining* involvement throughout childhood and into adulthood. Or put another way: "Childhood privilege in and of itself does not give a leg-up on entrepreneurship and innovation. Arts and crafts apparently do."

# The Arts in Childhood: Critical for Innovation

A number of factors diminish children's opportunities for participation in the arts. As one recent research project suggests, parents often aren't aware of the tangible benefits of activities like arts and crafts. Richard teamed with Elmer's Products to survey more than 300 moms (with children between three and eight years of age) to determine their perceptions of the benefits and barriers of arts and crafts. One key finding was that while moms *understand* that arts and crafts can have cognitive benefits, the vast majority would like to hear more about the unique developmental payoffs. So we conducted a study with a number of child development experts to explore the developmental benefits of arts and crafts. Many were identified, and here we mention three key findings and simultaneously offer direct tips for parenting:

> » *Promoting imaginative thinking.* We know now that a fundamental part of innovative thinking is imagining what's *not* there. Crafting—whether you are following instructions or doing something free form—gives kids a chance to imagine what they are going to create *before* they create it. As a parent, encourage this kind of thinking with questions (keep it fun; it's not a test) and reinforce your child's own talk about what they are thinking.

» *Encouraging the thinking that leads to problem solving.* Crafting allows kids not merely to imagine a possible future, but to make a plan to bring it to fruition. Making the problem-solving steps transparent—and encouraging kids to talk about this in an engaging way—reinforces the development of this important skill. The internal reward that comes from experiencing an "aha" moment also strongly reinforces innovative thinking.

» *Reinforcing the "doing" part of problem solving.* Crafting takes kids all the way through the creative process. The more hands-on, the better. This supports fine motor development but also the linkage between fine motor skills, visual processing, and higher-order cognitive work. Here the idea of "less is more" parenting is especially important. Let them try out gluing a dog's ear where the nose should be. Give them a chance to examine it and change it if they want to. If they want to deviate from the instructions, give them the opportunity to do so, and let them determine how that worked out.

Such open-ended activities encourage what researchers refer to as divergent thinking—the ability to "think outside the box," challenge the established ways of looking at things, and generate cognitive alternatives rather than the prescribed and expected.

You can think of this skill as a more mature manifestation of the cognitive skills used to support counterfactual reasoning. The website Edutopia.org—a site run by the George Lucas Educational Foundation (GLEF)—has published an informative blog post titled "Fueling Creativity in the Classroom with Divergent Thinking," which reviews how divergent thinking can be underused in classrooms (for example, demanding one and only one answer to a question, making students scared to be "wrong") and why it should be encouraged in children's formative experiences. The arts provide a wonderful opportunity for children to engage in their own divergent thinking, in part because they are typically so open-ended.

As a parent, you can foster divergent thinking in many ways. Think about all those times your child asks a question and you feel tempted to supply the answer. Turning the Q&A of parent-child interaction into an open-ended discussion is a great way to foster divergent thinking. It can happen with any topic at any time. "Why are we stuck in traffic?" your child asks. Generate the obvious and less obvious answers and try to get your child to do the same: It's rush hour; too many people work the same hours; too many companies are located in the same area; we don't have enough alternate routes; more people should carpool. How many solutions can your child come up with? While the arts often demand divergent thinking, the reality is that life does, too.

## Connecting the Dots

By being encouraged to explore a lot of different things without pressure to pick one to excel at, Rachel Brooks, the award-winning innovator and cofounder of Citizen Made, had a large palette of information available for integration into her pathway to innovation. For her, the pursuit of many interests led to a way of thinking that made connections across different domains. Brooks's cognitive "hook" was learning to detect *patterns*—something she discovered in art, music, fashion, advertising, and computer coding. The concept of the "pattern" gave her a template for understanding many ideas and also integrating her thinking across her seemingly disparate domains. Music and sewing and drawing and painting weren't all discrete, disconnected skills—music might motivate what clothes you wanted to make, while aspects of drawing connected to the physical process of sewing. For example, when Brooks wanted to learn Spanish, she began listening to Spanish songs. "Listening to the music helped connect me to the new words and their meaning. And the physical act of writing out the lyrics and hearing the music in my head certainly facilitated my ability to process this new vocabulary and grammar."

Brooks appreciates that she had an opportunity to develop a way of looking at things abstractly: "When you start to see patterns, you begin to think about how patterns intersect. You begin to cultivate a broader way of thinking that spurs creativity. What are the patterns and the voids in patterns that I can fill to make something I'm working on more interesting? In other words, how do I make it better? I later applied that thinking when I graduated college and started to make connections for myself between computer programming and developing tools to help people design their own products in concert with the people who made the products. It was my own connection across domains that I explored to see if I could make something that would be not only interesting but valuable to someone."

Jen's experience as an entrepreneur, and her many opportunities to collaborate with and observe other entrepreneurs, leads her to a similar way of thinking. She regularly sees that the most creative people intentionally forge connections between disparate parts of observed reality. In this way, they often find the opportunities hidden in adversity and failure. When Jen joined forces with her partner Dan Jacobs in 1992, everything about the opportunity seemed wrong. Jen wanted a job in the big city, while the opportunity Dan offered her was in the suburbs. She wanted to work at a big firm; Dan's firm was a start-up. She wanted to work on prestigious client accounts; the start-up had none. But Jen had graduated in a recession and the big PR agencies in New York had implemented hiring freezes. So she joined the unattractive start-up, and instead of complaining, she asked herself: "How can I make this what I want it to be?" Connecting a number of dots, she realized there was a hidden opportunity in her market. The big firms were putting their A teams on the "sexy clients," leaving less sexy clients such as insurance companies, industrial firms, energy companies, and others to be served by subpar players. Jen decided to focus and dig in. She built something unexpected: a firm that put "boring" clients on a pedestal. She took that company from three employees to almost a hundred.

In the book *The Innovator's DNA: Mastering the Five Skills of Disruptive Innovators*, Jeff Dyer, Hal Gregerson, and Clayton M. Christensen interviewed 100 innovative entrepreneurs about important skills that support entrepreneurial success. Among the skills that came up was "associating," that is, making connections across many, often unrelated fields. Many companies today encourage "associating" by creating "open" offices where colleagues can bump into one another and make fortuitous connections in the course of a day. For her part, Jen enjoys hearing all this buzz in her firm's open-plan offices; if cross-pollination of ideas happens ten times a day, she argues, the firm has generated ten new ideas that would have never occurred in a traditional office sitting.

By giving children opportunities for "associating" at home, we prepare them better for the future that awaits them. Let kids follow their inner muses. Let them be samplers rather than specialists so that they can get in the habit of integrating information in unique ways. Talk to them about their emerging interests. See if they can start to articulate, as they get older, their own connections about their growing passions. Ask them questions and let them offer expansive, open-ended answers. Here modern technology is a great tool, offering kids access to all sorts of information about their passions. Encourage them to find out more about what they like and share it with you. Reinforce the excitement they feel when they do this. It's notable that an emerging trend is for millennials is to be "career jugglers" not by necessity, but by choice. Sheila Marikar, writing in the *New York Times*, provides an interesting glimpse into the multiple careers that those of the "slash generation" (as in lawyer/guitarist) actively pursue. It's not necessary to limit oneself to only one career, not just in the chronological sense, but also in real time.

Also keep in mind that author Rick Newman has provided evidence suggesting that "conceptualization"—the art of seeing the big picture and connecting dots others don't connect—is the most important "überskill" that promotes success in any field. Newman makes the point that the best conceptualizers possess this skill in part by being attuned to lots of different types of information (not just their area of expertise) and develop the skill and habit of being able to make associations that elude others and lead to innovation—and illustrates the point by discussing how conceptualization can lead to success in any number of careers.

Starting in their early teens, your kids will begin to spend more and more time alone in their room. This is their incubator—a place in which they can surround themselves with all their interests. Encourage this immersion, for this is how they will start to practice connecting the dots. Hanging out with friends provides another dimension, offering them the social context in which to share their interests and hear more about what their friends are into, sparking even more connections. You might think they are just hanging out, but in truth they're also *integrating* all the influences that will make them unique—and uniquely successful.

# 3

RAISING OPTIMISTS

If there is one trait associated with entrepreneurs, it's optimism. Countless articles in the popular press have affirmed optimism's importance for entrepreneurs, as do a number of research papers. But it's also become fashionable to suggest that entrepreneurs can be *too* optimistic—and that such an "optimism bias" can lead them to fail. So is optimism a good or a bad trait for entrepreneurs?

Each year for more than a decade, Swedish citizens were asked to gauge the state of their economy over the past twelve months and to make predictions about the next twelve months. Analyzing this data set, researchers at Lund University found that entrepreneurs had a rosier perspective on the prior year than the rest of the population, as well as a more positive forecast for the year to come. But was this positive viewpoint unrealistic? Well, the entrepreneurs' perceptions and predictions fit the actual economic data *better* than that of other survey respondents. William Frick, writing in the *Harvard Business Review* blog, offered his succinct take on this research: "Entrepreneurs don't have an optimism bias—you have a pessimism bias."

Optimists are sometimes disparaged as "seeing the world through rose-colored glasses" and "viewing the glass as half full," but it may be that they are more attuned to reality than pessimistic thinkers. Psychologists Charles S. Carver and Michael F. Scheier—arguably the most influential scholars on optimism over the past few decades—cast a nuanced eye on the available research, suggesting that an *optimal* level of optimism exists, one that is high but not too extreme. As Carver and Scheier emphasize, optimism as a trait has both a cognitive component (the idea that future outcomes will be positive) and a motivational component ("optimistic people exert effort, whereas pessimistic people disengage from effort"). The power of thinking positive doesn't derive from the notion that good things will magically happen, but rather from the belief that *an application of appropriate effort* can take a given situation and make it better. Action matters. To the extent that optimists actually get up and do things, they enjoy a real advantage. And that advantage starts at home.

## "Life Is Good"

John Jacobs, cofounder (with his brother Bert) and chief creative optimist of the "Life is good" lifestyle brand, exemplifies the optimist's advantages. In 1989, he and Bert designed their first product, a T-shirt. With no business training or plan, they started selling their T-shirts on the streets of Boston and in college dormitories along the East Coast. For five long years, the brothers barely scraped by, sleeping in their van and surviving on peanut butter and jelly sandwiches. Then in 1994, they designed a T-shirt featuring a character named Jake. Jake was nothing more than a "somewhat crudely drawn elongated smiley face with a huge grin and jaunty beret" that conveyed a simple, optimistic message: "Life is good." This was a fundamental principle in the brothers' lives, one they believed in and followed on a daily basis. The Jake shirt was an immediate hit, with all forty-eight of the first batch sold in one afternoon. Today, Life is good is a $100 million company built around that same authentic message of optimism.

A skeptic might claim that hugely successful entrepreneurs can promote optimism because their life *is* good. But the Jacobs brothers' lives *weren't* all that easy when they first started their business, and optimism—believing that their lives were good even though times were tough—helped them make it through. This leads us to an interesting question: Where did all that positivity come from? John Jacobs told us that he credits his parents, explaining how he and his brother did not grow up with many advantages. Their childhood home was "chaotic"—six kids growing up in a small house—yet thanks to his parents, the emotional climate of the house was unquestionably positive. "There was plenty to complain about if you wanted to, yet it seemed like when we woke up in our bunk beds, we'd hear our mom singing or cracking up over something. She just decided to focus on things that made her laugh or things that would be exciting to her kids. There was no dwelling on the fact that the toast was burning again or that one of the kids was wearing cleats to school because they couldn't find their shoes.

"This idea of what you choose to focus on is one of the most basic foundations for a happy life for you and your kids," John Jacobs told us. "Do you want your child growing up thinking how lucky he or she is and how incredible this world is and how many opportunities there are every day to do things that are new, and to grow as a person? This isn't corny to me; it's what I truly believe."

It's what we believe, too—and what the latest child development research confirms. Since being optimistic constitutes a real career and life advantage, parents are wise to take steps to instill it in their children. Simply by creating a positive environment at home, parents can help children become more resilient, happy, and energetic as they get older.

## Is Happy Parenting Possible?

At first glance, such contentions might seem difficult to believe due to a grim pessimism that has taken hold of parenting culture. Lylah M. Alphonse, senior editor of "Yahoo! Shine," wondered in a blog post if parents who hate parenting are "the latest trend." Jennifer Senior's bestselling book *All Joy and No Fun: The Paradox of Modern Parenthood* also depicts raising children as a daily grind that can be exhausting and emotionally depleting.

Of course, parenting *can* be challenging and stressful—for any number of reasons. Every parent has had a day when nearly everything goes wrong. *But unpleasantness and hardship aren't the dominant part of the parenting experience*, as some commentators suggest. Richard (in collaboration with other researchers) has studied thousands of parents through interviews, questionnaires, and observational research. His findings reveal a vast range in the quality and dynamics of the parent-child relationship. Some parents portrayed an overall positive parenting experience; despite daily hassles and challenges, they maintained a fundamentally positive style of interaction with their children. Other parents didn't seem as satisfied, and had much more negative interactions with their children. From such interactions, a family climate is established, which impacts how positively or negatively youth feel about themselves.

You may wonder if genetics plays a key role: Are people just born optimists or pessimists? Do happy parents carry some type of protective DNA that immunizes them against the pressures of parenting? Not really. Richard has conducted a number of studies of how depression "runs" in families, which take into account the impact of genes along with the environment. Do genes matter in these studies? Yes, but the effect is not as strong as some may think—in fact, the environment provides as much (if not more) explanatory power as genetic effects. Genes are much less deterministic than they are made out to be for most emotional and behavioral disorders and traits.

Genetically informed studies of optimism over the past few decades bear this out. Australian researchers examined nearly 4,000 pairs of adult twins—some identical and some fraternal—asking them to rate their levels of optimism. They then calculated the degree to which optimism is "inherited." For women, genetics accounted for between 27 and 47 percent of the trait; for men it was only 8 to 19 percent. Environmental factors, which in principle include rearing environment and life experiences, played the strongest role in shaping optimists and pessimists.

## Early Parenting Matters

Scientists and clinicians have long believed that babies enter the world with their own temperaments or personalities. Parents often think so, too. Some babies are easygoing and seem to roll with most things; others are more demanding and difficult. Over the decades, a long list of studies support the notion that genetic factors do, in part, shape temperamental characteristics, and evidence suggests that personality is not inherited in the classic sense. Yes, genes shape a child's propensity to be emotionally reactive versus laid-back, but the child's environment matters, too—arguably *much more* than many think.

An influential study published in 2011 demonstrates this principle clearly, as it showed how negative parenting can take a happy baby and turn him or her into an angry, negative child. Researchers Michael Lorber and Byron Egeland examined data tracking 267 babies from the first week of life through first grade. They wanted to see how cranky, highly irritable babies would respond to positive (warm and supportive) parenting as opposed to negative (hostile and angry) parenting. Would difficult infants become angry and misbehaving kids when they entered school only when they received negative parenting?

Trained observers recorded the behavior of babies at seven and ten weeks old, rating their levels of irritability. Then they visited the families when the babies were three and six months old and asked the moms to rate how difficult or pleasant they thought the babies were. During these visits, the research team observed the moms themselves during feeding time, rating them on how much cuddling and cooing they provided as well as the amount of anger, frustration, and disgust they displayed.

Finally, the researchers brought the moms and babies to a university laboratory when the babies were two and three-and-a-half years old. They gave each mom and toddler a series of puzzles that grew in difficulty, videotaping their behavior. Researchers noted varying signs of hostility in the moms, including anger, rejection, and discounting their toddler's ideas on how to solve tasks. They also recorded how angry the toddlers were and counted how many times *they* rejected their moms' input.

The results told an interesting story. Moms and toddlers

tended to be very "mutual" in their behavior; when one was negative, so was the other—and likewise for positive behavior. But contrary to predictions, *the babies' early temperament told researchers almost nothing about which mom-toddler pairs had the most negative interactions.* What made a difference was the amount of positivity and negativity the mom displayed when the babies were three and six months old. Difficult, cranky babies who received a lot of affection from their moms were likely to enjoy a good relationship with their mom during the toddler years (the notorious "terrible twos"). Easygoing babies who received lots of maternal negativity ended up having a mutually contentious relationship with their moms as toddlers. No matter how they came into the world, the toddlers ended up acting a lot like their moms.

The research team continued to study these children as they grew older and began formal schooling. The results were stunning. Kids who had a predominantly negative relationship with Mom suffered significantly more problems in school. They acted out more, lost control of their behavior, and were physically aggressive. The big message is this: Parental negativity during infancy can impact a child's later behavior. A baby who enters the world as a happy, easygoing bundle of joy can morph into an angry, misbehaving "problem child" just five years later if negativity dominates the parent-child relationship. The power of parental emotions and

> Parental negativity during infancy can impact a child's later behavior.

the tone of the family climate can not only shape but also override a child's "inborn" tendency to be more or less happy.

## The Emotional Roots of Optimism

While it is hardly revolutionary to suggest that a positive rearing environment is preferable to a negative one, the connection with optimism has been less widely appreciated. We can glimpse the effect parents have on optimism by studying how a toddler or young child handles frustration, specifically that stemming from a difficult or challenging task. How do children learn to regulate their feelings when something is hard to master, gaining the cognitive "fuel" to persist and not give up? Entrepreneurs succeed precisely because they possess such cognitive fuel. Even when the odds are stacked against them in starting a business, they persist because they believe they can beat the odds and make something good happen. They focus on finding what they can change, guiding their behavior in productive ways. This is what we usually mean when we describe entrepreneurs as "optimistic."

For decades, researchers have turned to "hard puzzle" tasks as a window into toddlers' emerging ability to persevere in the face of challenges. In research studies, toddlers are given puzzles of varying degrees of difficulty, and scholars observe their behavior and emotions. Some toddlers will stay on the task with determined effort and regulated emotion, working on the puzzle until they figure it out or are told that they can stop. Other kids get distracted once they realize they will not be able to solve the puzzle quickly. Still others will grow frustrated at the outset and disengage from the task entirely.

These differences in children's reactions matter; they strongly predict academic readiness and classroom behavior. Kids who can control the negative emotions associated with frustration and exhibit a more positive, determined outlook are more prepared for challenges they are likely to face in school. You may wonder if they are less frustrated simply because they are better at doing puzzles than their peers. That's why researchers include puzzles that can't be solved—the idea is to gauge their tolerance for a difficult situation that will not lead to success.

Researchers also observe how *parents* respond when their children are presented with "hard puzzle" tasks. Bear in mind, the parents are not "in" on the experiment—all they know is that their child is going to do some puzzles and that they can offer support however they like. Some parents acknowledge that the puzzles are difficult and encourage their children to keep trying, others get annoyed with their children's inability to complete the puzzles, and some will even criticize their children for not figuring it out.

At moments like this in a child's life, parents can lay the groundwork for optimistic thinking—even during the toddler years. They can accustom a child to stick with something even when it's not panning out. When a child is struggling, parents shouldn't pretend that everything is going great or that a miracle will happen out of nowhere. Optimism isn't about such "magical" thinking. Rather, it's about accepting or even embracing the challenges and trying to figure out how to handle them—what researchers call "frustration tolerance." Getting angry or upset as a parent and letting those emotions spin out of control lead children to become less persistent, undermining their ability to learn and handle challenges.

Parents can observe their children and assess how prone they are to unhelpful frustration. Kids who become frustrated—and it usually happens fast—should be guided to calm down; overtly remind them that while it's natural to get frustrated, it's important to stay with it. Also, keep an eye out for the child who simply withdraws from a challenge. Disengagement is also a signal of frustration—and again, encouragement is necessary. Break it down for them. If we are talking about a puzzle, give some tips about how to look for pieces that might fit.

Take some time to reflect on how *you* model persistence. Do you fly off the handle when something is difficult? Do you groan and complain? Slam things down? Say things like "Forget it!" and storm off? Remember that your children are observing you and potentially modeling your behavior. Your child has many academic, social, and personal challenges ahead of him. Some assignments, tests, and entire courses will be hard. He might face difficulties with kids at school. He might fail at first in sports or art or music. Modeling a proactive way of dealing with challenges—a belief that you can figure something out if you go at it systematically and deliberately—helps kids persist in their own lives. They learn that it pays to stay positive and stick with something—lessons that can make a great difference in success and life.

## Optimistic Parents Help Children Endure Adversity

As adults, we know that the optimist's edge pays off most when a person faces great adversity—divorce, economic hardship, serious illness. One reason, as we have seen, is that optimists excel at understanding the *reality* of their situation. They acknowledge the realities so they can find something—anything—to make their life better. As psychologists Carver and Scheier have written: "[O]ptimists . . . do not simply stick their heads in the sand and ignore threats to well-being. . . . Optimists may be more confident than pessimists that their efforts will be successful. For that reason, they are quicker to engage those efforts when there is a need for them."

Does this principle really apply to parenting? A team of scientists tracked the progress of nearly 400 ten-year-olds growing up in single-mother households that were experiencing substantial economic pressure. The average family income of these households was around $20,000 per year, well below the national average. These researchers wanted to see how tough economic times created family stress, and how the children were affected over time.

Three times over a six-year period, researchers asked moms and kids to fill out questionnaires. Moms reported on how stressed, anxious, or depressed they felt; they also indicated how angry or loving they felt toward their child, along with how involved they were in their children's daily lives (for example, the extent to which they helped with homework). Their children's experiences were also collected; they reported on how affectionate their mom was as well as how much their mom criticized them or got angry. The research team *also* gathered data on the kids' behavior in school and their academic performance.

As you might expect, stress hit many of these struggling moms hard. Many of them were depressed, would get angry and critical around their sons and daughters, showed less affection, had trouble taking care of their children's emotional needs, and didn't manage their children's behavior very well. *Yet not every family reacted negatively over the six-year period, even though they had the same economic burdens.* Some parents seemed to ride out the economic storm well—and this served their children well. The moms in these families were better able to help foster learning and growth by supporting their children's homework. Their children performed well academically and remained enthusiastic about school. They also did better emotionally and socially, with fewer behavioral problems.

The "X factor" that distinguished these moms from others was their high level of optimism. These moms expected good things to happen even during uncertain and difficult times; they maintained positive family interactions, limited their own hostility, and tended to their children's needs. Their kids grew into teenagers with strong emotional and social skills, kids who were motivated to stay in school and succeed. Maternal optimism is indeed a powerful buffer against stress, protecting kids and keeping their development on track even when it has every reason to fall behind.

Researchers never rely on the findings of just one study, regardless of how well it is conducted. They know they're on to something when they can repeat a study with the same basic results. So it's important that another study used the same research approach with economically disadvantaged families in northern California—and arrived at the same conclusion. Even in the face of their economic struggle, optimistic moms in this second study also experienced less anxiety and depression, were more involved in their children's lives, and raised healthy, happy kids who were more engaged and successful in school.

These studies should be inspiring to parents faced with adversity; they suggest that parents can still have a major, positive impact on their children even during the worst of times. And let's face it: At some point, almost every family is faced with some type of misfortune. During those inevitable hardships, it helps to know that you can still be doing something effective for your child's development. Optimistic people always find aspects of their life they can control and then work to make those elements better. Parents can, too.

## Parenting for Success:
## Support Versus Harshness

For all the advantages of supporting children who face hardship, isn't it more important to push kids hard to succeed in a highly competitive world? If you don't demand a lot from them, won't they slack off? Doesn't all that indulgent stuff just make kids lazy and unsuccessful?

Amy Chua has made the phrase "tiger mom" ubiquitous in the parenting world, to the point of seeming almost cartoonish. But Chua's notion of how much we should demand of our children reflects a common view. For some youth, academic stress is off the charts—a situation that has long prevailed at top universities. Richard recalls his freshman year in college at Yale. Cell phones didn't exist then; students shared one phone, typically set up in a dormitory hallway, which made private conversations somewhat public. Many students held weekly conversations with parents; these often devolved into loud, stressful assurances that the kids were busting their tails to get the best grades possible—as if there wasn't enough pressure from being in class with a bunch of students who had *also* received top grades in high school. One can imagine what the lives of some kids may be like now that every student has a cell phone.

Desiree Qin, professor of psychology at Michigan State University, has been studying parenting in Asian American families for almost a decade. Based on her research, Qin believes this style of parenting is not optimal for children's overall development: "When children receive more pressure and get pestered to achieve more than their peers, they report higher levels of conflicts and less emotional warmth and closeness with their parents. Not surprisingly, they are less happy—indeed, they are more likely to be depressed and anxious, and have low self-esteem."

Some children of "tiger parents" *do* go on to experience great success in school, but they often also carry significant emotional scars. In one of her papers, Qin examined two groups of high-achieving kids: One group was distressed, the other mentally healthy. The primary factor differentiating these two groups was *parenting*, as better mental health outcomes were associated with factors like spending time with children and giving children a sense of freedom. Qin's work demonstrates how happy kids with good parental relationships can succeed at the highest level, without emotional baggage.

Let's go back to that freshman year at Yale. Almost every student had to make emotional adjustments, regardless of their background. College was a new game with new players and the level of competition was raised to the highest level. No one was the "smartest kid in class" anymore—just about everybody was. Adapting to that situation required a certain emotional and cognitive flexibility *and* a sense that one was equipped to handle setbacks and adversity. All kids need to have some level of optimism so they can push through bumps in the road when they hit them. Universities are beginning to realize this. The Massachusetts Institute of Technology (MIT)—one of the most rigorous universities in the world—has implemented a new policy in which no grades are given during the first semester of freshman year. This allows first-year students a chance to adjust to college's demands without immediate pressures and punitive reinforcement (that is, bad grades). They need time in order to figure out how to adapt in a positive way. Parents can serve their children well by providing similar opportunities to adjust and adapt positively. This lays the foundation for later successes in the most competitive environments.

## Optimistic—and Pessimistic— Ways of Thinking

So far, we've focused on optimism's emotional component. But, of course, there is a strong *cognitive* dimension as well. Let's begin with the first stage of childhood. Recall the studies mentioned earlier that focused on parents' emotions and how babies/toddlers react to them. It turns out that those experiences can predict whether babies will develop optimistic or pessimistic approaches to life. John Jacobs, founder of Life is good, understood this intuitively when we asked him if he thought of himself as an optimist during his childhood: "I'm sure I didn't know the word for it, or even understood what optimism meant. But I think myself and my siblings could feel it in the house and we'd look to my mom for that. We grew up having the spirit of enjoying the ride as we go. We'd gravitate to other people that make you laugh and lift you up."

That's how it happens. All that early exposure to positivity sets up a template for a kid to think like an optimist—even before he or she *knows* what optimism is. Remember, we are talking about a realistic type of optimism—not Pollyannaish avoidance—that focuses on what can be done in the moment to make something better. A child's brain registers everything during the early years of life and fashions it into a habitual way of approaching the world: "Maybe not everything is great right now, but what can I do to improve it? What is under my control?"

Researchers at the University of Notre Dame found that kids (in second through ninth grade) who grow up with pervasive parental negativity demonstrate negative emotions like sadness, withdrawal, and sometimes anger. As they grow, especially through middle school and during the transition to high school, they tend to develop "a negative attribution style." That is, they come to *expect* bad things to happen to them and they find it difficult to see the positives that might be embedded in negative situations. They don't think they have it *in themselves* to make good things happen. Conversely, when bad things happen, they are convinced that they are to blame. In contrast, researchers found that kids with positive parental experiences thought differently about themselves and the world: They saw themselves as capable of making good things happen and also believed in their ability to make the best out of bad situations. They understood that adversity called for doing something positive with a challenge.

As you might expect, kids who develop a positive attributional style are much better equipped to weather life's down moments during their vulnerable teenage years. A study in Australia followed more than 5,600 teens from eighth grade through tenth grade; the kids high on optimism had *half the risk for depression* by tenth grade. At these ages, children's overt cognitive style begins to form, and how parents express themselves tells children a lot about how parents see the world. As a parent, do you convey that you have no control over the events in your life, particularly the negative ones? Do you always say there is "nothing you can do" to improve difficulties at work? No steps to take to impact your finances?

Now, we are not suggesting it's beneficial to avoid talking about difficulties you may be experiencing altogether, pretending that everything is great when it isn't. Plenty of studies show, for example, that optimists recover better than pessimists from health challenges; they simply comply better with small steps that must be taken on the long road to recovery. So modeling for your child *positive* cognitions about the realities of life sends the message that you can always find ways to make something good happen.

This kind of talk is also necessary when your kids talk about their own lives. Kids experience all kinds of challenges, including many that involve elements beyond their control. Maybe they have a teacher whom they don't connect with, and the result is consistently bad grades. Think about how you might discuss this. You could say "life is tough" and tell them to suck it up; you could say that you will get them another teacher; *or* you could say that this happens sometimes and will probably happen again in the future, emphasizing that it's important to try to find ways to make the situation better. If you choose the last of these approaches, you could ask the teacher to meet with you and your child to identify specific things that can be done in the classroom and/or at home. You could also talk about getting a tutor. Either way, you are sending a message that you understand the realities of the situation and that it's important to consider what can improve the situation. This approach to challenges and setbacks *empowers* children to think about what's under their control without creating unrealistic expectations.

## When Does Optimistic Thinking Take Hold?

Researchers at the University of California, Davis, have broken new ground in studying the development of optimism. They wanted to see if kids applied optimistic thinking to real-life situations and *when* this typically happens during childhood. They presented children (between the ages of five and ten) with illustrated scenarios in which two characters experienced the same event, but thought differently about it—one had positive thoughts, the other negative thoughts. Some of the events depicted were positive, and some negative. Here's an example of a negative scenario:

*Two kids are riding a two-person bike. The bike falls over and they both break their arms. One kid says this is cool because they will get casts that their friends can sign. The other kid says that the cast will be itchy and it will be hard to play.*

Children then had to explain what each character thought and why they thought that way; they also had to rate how each of the characters felt and *why* they felt differently. While all children could identify differences in the emotions of the two characters, older kids offered explanations that revealed awareness of the construct of optimism. When explaining the broken arm scenario, one child responded: "She's thinking on the positive side and that's good . . . because there's nothing you can do about it; she's just trying to make the best of it."

Kids' explanations didn't just depend on their ages, but also on how optimistic they judged *themselves* to be. Kids who rated themselves low on optimism (by responding to a questionnaire that probed for underlying indicators) knew that the characters experienced different emotions, but didn't see anything wrong when a character had a negative reaction to a positive event. In contrast, kids who rated themselves high on optimism understood more keenly the distinction between the characters and could easily tell that negative characters were prone to bringing negativity into their life; they sniffed out pessimism as something that traps you and should be avoided. By age ten, these kids were already making the connection that some attitudes make bad things better, while others only make bad situations worse. This study yielded another big finding: *The best predictor of which kids thought and spoke like an optimist was the level of optimism in their parents.*

Kids really do soak up emotions and cognitions from their parents. They learn to view challenging situations either optimistically or pessimistically, whether it's a difficult puzzle presented to toddlers in the laboratory or economic adversity during the school years. And by time they hit middle childhood, they have formed cognitive representations of how the world works ("Will things always be bad?" versus "Is there something good that's gonna happen to me?") and how effective they will be in taking on adversity ("Is this a hole I can't climb out of?" versus "Is there something I can do to make this even a little bit better right now?").

## Frame the Day with Positive Thinking

The material we've presented certainly speaks to the importance of the emotional and cognitive climate of families. Looking deeper, we find that family climate is often reflected and influenced by how families *start the day*. Richard has conducted a number of workshops with families who are trying to find new ways to break the cycle of conflict, argument, and negativity. Without exception, every family could articulate the trigger for a "bad day," and it would always happen first thing in the morning. Perhaps one child made sure he finished off a box of cereal before a sibling could have any. Perhaps one child took too long to get ready. Whatever started it, the net result was a negative attitude right at the start of the day that was hard to shake. Many parents even referred to this as their "morning routine."

Think about how *you* start your day. Do you stress out thinking about all the things you have to get done and the "bad things" awaiting you? Or do you treat the day as an opportunity to do something positive, mobilizing yourself to take on challenges and possible setbacks? The way you start your day is also the way your child will start his or her day.

> The way you start your day is also the way your child will start his or her day.

When Jen was a child, her father had a pretty unusual daily habit. At some point each morning, he would stride to the kitchen window, throw it open, and shout at the top of his lungs: "Hello, world! What a beautiful day! Thank you for this day!" If Jen happened to have friends over when this happened, she cringed with embarrassment. Other days, she was happy her family lived on four acres of land in a rural town, where no one could hear him. But when she looks back on her dad's behavior, she understands what he was up to. If you start the day with appreciation, you have a better shot at actually having a good day. This attitude becomes infectious and steers you to look for good moments and opportunities that may come your way, as opposed to getting hung up on minor setbacks.

John Jacobs, cofounder and chief creative optimist of Life is good, recalls waking up each day to the sound of his mother's joyous singing. He, too, suggests that his parents set an emotional climate for each day: "I love the word 'excited.' It can be used every day when you wake up! You can talk in an excited voice about the color of the trees today or what the sky looks like. It's a decision you make on how you are going to frame your day from morning to night."

In Richard's workshops, families were asked to identify morning triggers that would lead to negativity and to brainstorm ways to eliminate them. After trying different approaches in the home, parents who succeeded in reducing family stress found that what worked best was introducing positive expectations rather than trying to manage the negative. For example, one mom started a routine in which before bed, each child identified something they were looking forward to the next day. Mom would then write it down on an index card, and in the morning, she'd leave the card next to each child's breakfast, asking them to shout out why they were going to have a good day. It was a fun way for her kids to frame their day and allow positive emotion to squeeze out room that might otherwise be inhabited by negative feelings.

It's so easy to get into the habit of starting the day with negatives. The optimist's edge is to *unearth the positives*. Starting off the day with a positive feeling is great for a child heading out for school—and the same thinking applies to the end of the work/school day. So many parents and kids invest time and energy in wrapping up the day with complaints—what went wrong, what was hard, what was annoying. By contrast, consider Jacobs's experiences growing up: "My mom would do things like saying at the dinner table, 'Tell me something good that happened today.' It's so simple, but it really does frame the day in a positive light. Instead of feeling down or saying 'this teacher was tough' or 'this assignment is really hard,' you end up recapping something fun that happened at recess or something you thought was cool that you learned in class. And even if it's one thing, that might carry the conversation for twenty minutes . . . I think it's very powerful."

> The optimist's edge is to *unearth the positives.*

## Cultivate Gratitude

An important way to create a household that embraces optimism is by expressing *gratitude* and teaching your kids to do the same. Gratitude focuses us on what we have rather than what we don't have. That's why it's closely linked to optimism—it epitomizes the "glass is half full" perspective. Family dinners offer a daily routine for encouraging gratitude. It's a time when everyone is together, and as such offers a family-wide setting to talk about the day and the good things that can be recognized. Consider the experiences of Jacobs, whose family finds this practice rewarding. "Before dinner every person at our table shares what they are grateful for. Our four-year-old has taken over the leadoff slot. He likes to start the conversation and usually he just keeps going—it's good stuff! He'll say things like, 'I'm grateful for the floor, for the ceiling, for the lights, the ocean, and the color green.'" Jacobs offers a parallel observation about gratitude and the importance of embracing and practicing it in his company: "It's so simple, but it's a way of framing where you're at in your life right now. It's definitely one of the pillars of our company."

Jen also grew up in a very grateful household; in particular, her parents felt thankful to live in a country that afforded so much opportunity. Both her parents had been born in countries where getting ahead was reserved for a preselected few; so they reminded their kids on a daily basis that life is tougher in other parts of the world, and that the ability to achieve should be cherished. Jen believes her parents were trying to raise kids with the spirit and energy to capitalize on that potential. It's not surprising that gratitude and optimism often go hand in hand.

Significant research supports the benefits of gratitude and its close association with optimism. Dr. Robert Emmons, a leader in gratitude research, details several influential findings from his studies as follows:

» In an experimental comparison, those who kept gratitude journals exercised more regularly, reported fewer problematic physical symptoms, felt better about their lives as a whole, and were more optimistic about the upcoming week compared to those who recorded hassles or neutral life events.

» Participants who kept gratitude lists were more likely to make progress toward important personal goals (academic, interpersonal, and health based) over a two-month period, compared to subjects in other experimental conditions.

» Children who practice grateful thinking have more positive attitudes toward school and their families.

While it's not difficult to practice gratitude, it does require a certain psychological commitment. That is why it's a good practice to find time in the day in which you establish a "gratitude routine" with your kids. It can be at dinnertime, it can be at bedtime, it can be right when you wake up—the critical thing is to find a way to make it an expected part of every day.

## No More Boredom

Entrepreneurial thinkers aren't just effective at finding silver linings. They also go out of their way to figure out how they can make good things happen, which is another dimension of optimism. This trait can be fostered throughout childhood, and a good place to start is to take on the familiar refrain of "I'm bored" and replace it with a reminder that children don't have to *wait* for good things to happen. When boredom becomes pervasive, it often goes hand in hand with a dreary, enervated experience of the world. Jen remembers that declaring she was bored was one of the *biggest* offenses in her childhood home. A single "I'm bored" landed her with an assignment to accomplish something or do something productive—draw a picture or invent a new game. Jacobs offers a similar recollection from his childhood: "I remember distinctly my mom saying to us, 'The only people who get bored are boring people.' That was the last time I used the word 'bored'—when I was maybe six years old."

Sometimes kids need pumping up to generate enthusiasm. In the morning, when Jen's daughter is in an incorrigible mood and doesn't want to do anything (except watch television), Jen will get out crayons and start drawing a map. On that map is an adventure—the adventure of their day. Her daughter will grow curious and come over to investigate. "What are you doing, Mommy?" she asks. Jen draws a muffin and a glass of juice, a beach, an ice-cream cone, a gathering of people—anything that might happen in the day that can create excitement. Soon, her daughter will beam with excitement and Jen will reinforce it by saying, "Today's going to be a great day, isn't it?"

It's a reminder that they have an ability *within them* to make something good happen. Optimism isn't just about figuring out if the glass is half empty or half full. It's also about figuring out how you can fill up the glass yourself.

# 4

## Opportunity Seekers

Many parents today think back on freedoms they had that their children are now missing—like roaming around the neighborhood or hopping on a bike and riding somewhere without parental supervision or knowledge of where they were. While we took on this point when we discussed the need for exploration in a child's life, here we will approach the issue from another angle. It's been suggested that unfounded fears are unduly dissuading many parents today from allowing their children to do these things, thereby creating a generation of youth who are reluctant to take risks. For example, Hanna Rosin, writing in *The Atlantic*, claims that parents' perceptions of danger (such as injury or abduction by a stranger) just don't correspond to statistical reality. She argues that parents have developed an irrational risk aversion that inhibits children from doing nearly *anything* outside of the home—and as a result, children are being deprived of the chance to learn by experience and develop basic competencies.

A study published in *Pediatrics* converges with some of Rosin's points. Focus groups comprised of child care providers (for example, directors of preschools and day care centers) were conducted to explore barriers to children's participation in play. The providers reported that safety concerns expressed by parents (as well as administrative regulatory issues) substantially influenced them to inhibit children's time on the playground. But that's not all. Responding to parents' fears as well as the dictates of local and state governments, schools constructed playgrounds that were "too safe" for the age groups they were designed to serve—simply put, they were too boring to engage young children. It's worth adding the ironic footnote that giving children play equipment that is too juvenile *may* lead them to find ways to make it more interesting—by doing things they shouldn't be doing and getting hurt in the process. The National Childcare Accreditation Counsel of Australia has summarized this point succinctly: "Children are more likely to add or create risks or to engage in unsafe behavior when their environments are sterile or boring."

Rosin, like other observers, makes the point that too many parents today don't want their children taking risks, because they fear the consequences. But this risk-averse approach does a disservice to children, who need to experience risks and their possible negative fallouts in order to prepare themselves for the reality of the world that awaits them. There is speculation that kids who don't know how to take on everyday "risks" will not embrace all the risks one needs to take to be competitive in life—like how to pounce on a job opportunity or start a business. As Jen will tell you, that's a shortcoming that most entrepreneurs simply will not abide, and that could have serious consequences for your children as they grow and mature. But as we're about to explore, not all risks are created equal.

## Are Entrepreneurs Really Risk-Takers?

Conventional wisdom regards the entrepreneur as a risk-taker par excellence—people risking their life savings and playing high-stake games they sometimes win (big) and sometimes lose (big). While there are certainly plenty of stories on such high-stake risk-takers, we contend that many (if not most) highly successful entrepreneurs do not take indiscriminate risks. Instead, they favor a more informed and strategic approach. Malcolm Gladwell has argued, for example, that moguls such as Ted Turner built their enterprises specifically by *limiting* risk whenever they were making "bold" decisions. They certainly took their chances, but they made sure that the odds weren't stacked against them. Such a strategic approach generally protects them from catastrophic losses in case the venture doesn't pan out, positioning them to take on the next opportunity. Researchers Anna Macko and Tadeusz Tyszka also see entrepreneurial risk-taking as a process mediated by entrepreneurs' own skills and knowledge. While entrepreneurs cannot control all factors, they aren't just taking a chance or engaging in thrill-seeking behavior; they are making a calculated decision that factors in a lot of information, including *their unique ability* to improve the likelihood of a good outcome.

In one experiment, Macko and Tyszka recruited college students who were enrolled in a class on entrepreneurship because of a stated interest in starting a business; they recruited a second group of students who had no plans to be entrepreneurs, and a third group of same-age adults who were already entrepreneurs. All three groups completed two types of experimental tasks: One type gauged their inclination to take risks in a completely chance-driven game and the other measured their risk-taking behavior when they had an opportunity to apply information to their decisions. It turned out that entrepreneurs and entrepreneurs-in-training were no more prone to taking risks than others in a game of chance. *They were, however, bigger risk-takers when they had information that could guide their choices.* Macko and Tyszka sum up their findings this way: "We do not think that either inside or outside the laboratory entrepreneurs love risk more than other people. Perhaps, like the majority of humans, entrepreneurs try to avoid risks. Risky ventures which they undertake outside the laboratory are perhaps the result of a specific motivation and/or specific perception of risk involved in these ventures." What we propose is that entrepreneurs love to sniff out opportunities, and when they find them, they know how to take on and manage risk in order to maximize the likelihood of eventual success.

## Looking Before Leaping
## (and Having a Safety Net)

Jen's professional experience supports this conclusion. She has observed a range of risk-taking personalities throughout her career as an entrepreneur, but most successful people she has met took bets on *themselves* and their capabilities and had mechanisms for minimizing risk. Consider the founding of Jen's own company. Her original partner, Dan Jacobs, left his job at GE Capital and started a PR firm when he had three little kids and a mortgage. Jen was all of twenty-three years old and living in her parents' house, so making a decision to give up her steady job and partner with him was a less risky proposition for her (but a risk nonetheless). Jacobs, meanwhile, was banking on his extensive business experience and intuition that their vision for a PR firm would catch fire. It wasn't an indiscriminate risk, but one based on knowledge and some indication that it had a good chance of succeeding. Jacobs was very much looking before leaping, even if his risk might have seemed foolhardy to an outside observer.

Jen never considered herself to be a big risk-taker, but when she talks to other people, they think she is. In reality, she contends, she always secures whatever safety nets she can to minimize her chances of failure. When she went to business school at the age of twenty-five, she had to go into debt and move into her mother's basement in order to pay the $120,000 tuition, without any guarantee that it would pay off. Living in her mother's basement rather than paying rent served as a kind of safety net—if all else failed and she couldn't afford rent, she knew she would never go without a roof over her head. Jen's decision to open offices for her company in New York and London seemed risky, and perhaps it was. Still, she always made sure she took on the most conservative level of risk by subletting other people's offices in case her gamble didn't work out.

Throughout her business adventure, Jen has always felt that she could potentially predict the probability of success when she was taking on a risk. If that probability was around 75 percent, then she'd go for it, but if it was 10 percent, she wouldn't. She was able to forecast in part because she was betting on things that were partially if not largely under her control. She believed in herself, her experience, her vision, and her ability to execute on her plans while improvising to meet unanticipated circumstances. To her, that's not risk-taking but actually a feeling of exercising *control* over her destiny. Ask her if she wants to put a dollar in the stock market or a dollar in her own company, and she'll tell you she'd put the dollar in her own company any day because she feels that 75 percent of the time she knows how to make that dollar into two.

## Parental Perceptions of Risk-Taking

Thinking through parental perceptions of childhood risk is as nuanced a phenomenon as considering the role of "risk-taking" in the life of entrepreneurs. So much emphasis has been placed on *physical* risk facing our children that it makes sense to begin there. There *is* a lot of risk in the life of the young child. Sure, parents might overestimate some risks (like abduction) and inhibit their children excessively as a result. But as the influential pediatrician Dr. Harvey Karp suggests, we are also likely to *under*estimate risks. Karp observed that while some parents might feel anxious about their child swimming in the ocean (because of possible shark attack), some may leave their toddler unattended for just a few minutes in the backyard pool, not realizing that a toddler can drown in less than thirty seconds. Accidental drownings are the second leading cause of death in children between one and four years of age—and they frequently happen in home swimming pools.

Likewise, while we fear for our children's safety on the playground, we have been slow to acknowledge and act on the high rates of injury in children's organized sports. The risk for concussion in high school athletes has just *recently* begun to receive scrutiny, despite the fact that professional football has been illuminating the frequency, severity, and consequences of concussion for years. A study published in the *American Journal of Sports Medicine* suggests that the rate of concussion in high school athletes more than doubled between 2005 and 2012, primarily because of increased recognition. More than ever, parents are overtly weighing the probability of concussion when they sign their kids up for football or other sports; a poll indicates that over 40 percent of parents are now worried about the possibility of concussion. That said, only 5 percent are convinced to limit their children's football activities because of that concern. Maybe we are too afraid of the playground and the neighborhood, but it takes a lot of information to make us scared of the gridiron.

## Rethinking What We Mean by Risk-Taking

In thinking through risk-taking, we should remember that not every risk with children involves physical activities. Risk-taking is fundamentally a psychological phenomenon and it takes many forms. A student in a fourth grade class takes a risk when she raises her hand although she isn't sure she *knows* the answer to a question. An eighth grade student takes a risk when he tries out for a school play even though he's never acted before. A high school junior takes a risk when she signs up for a demanding literature elective that piques her interest even though the likelihood of getting an A may be low.

Our point in presenting these examples isn't to encourage risk-taking per se—it's to reframe our thinking as parents away from "risk-taking" as the inherent goal in favor of fostering an inclination to search out *opportunities* and learn how to manage their potential negative features or possible consequences. The fourth grader who raises her hand is proactively seeking new knowledge even though she may not look "smart" if she is "wrong." The eighth grader trying out for the play is living the idea that trying new things is a way to grow even if he isn't initially "good" at it. The high school junior is not letting the fear of a nonstellar grade impede her interest in literature. This is entrepreneurial thinking and behavior. Children can push themselves and reach for things without the paralyzing fear that something bad will happen, in part because *they* help define the boundaries. Think about it like this: If you are climbing a tree, there's a difference between trying to get to the next branch that's just out of reach (and taking the risk you will fall) and simply flinging yourself without any type of strategy.

The real goal, it seems, isn't to create a generation of random thrill seekers, but to cultivate children who have an entrepreneurial sense of how to seek out appropriate opportunities—academic, social, personal, and physical—without being thwarted by the possibility of "negative" consequences and paralyzed by fear. As parents, it may be helpful to consider ways of promoting thoughtful opportunity seeking in children. We need to create environments that *embrace* the inevitable failures our kids will encounter as they reach for that proverbial tree branch. And to a degree, the greater challenge for parents is to *accept* the necessity of that process. It may sound good in the abstract, but parents need to not only be ready with a Band-Aid when their children fall, but also be okay with something less than an A on a test.

## A Teacher Turns into an Entrepreneur

During his first year as an elementary school computer science teacher in Rhode Island, Alan Tortolani became frustrated by the lack of productive educational games on the web that he could utilize at school. The games available online seemed developmentally unhelpful, particularly those offered for free. Alan knew that "games had to be really fun, because engaging students is the first step to keeping their attention." He understood that kids use a number of senses as they play and may prefer one to others; games, therefore, should feature visual, auditory, and tactile components. They should also provide "clear navigational tools that are age-graded that would help children play with ease." And, of course, there had to be real intellectual content.

During that first year of teaching, Alan put his computer programming skills to work and started creating his own educational games to augment his teaching. By the end of the year, he had developed about twenty games. As he continued to develop more gaming content, he created apps that would allow the games to run on smartphones, tablets, and other mobile devices. Soon it was time for Alan to take a big leap. Continuing his creative work, he left his stable job to make a business out of his games. It was, he told us, "a scary thing to do. I had a very good job with long-term security, a pension, all those things you want in a job."

Alan's company, ABCya.com, has since become an influential and successful source for online educational games. ABCya

.com also offers numerous iPhone and iPad apps—all developed by Alan. There's a lesson in Alan's success. It would have been easier to just go with what programs were available or keep searching for games designed by others, but Alan created his *own* opportunities by reaching for the unknown, guided by his experience. We asked Alan if he could identify parts of his upbringing that may have contributed to his ability to seek out opportunity. He noted that he felt that he always "had a freedom to try things out without worrying about failure. This helped me find things that I liked and eventually the things I was good at, but in a very unstructured way. The key was that I could step out of my comfort zone." The message Alan received that he was free to "do his own thing" reverberated long past childhood. In college, he "took as many classes in lots of areas before I had to commit to a major. I wasn't worried about how that looked or how successful it would make me. I had 'permission' to take some chances without worrying about the consequences—especially during a period when I thought I should be exploring new areas."

Children thrive in environments like the one Alan grew up in—environments that push them out of their comfort zones, without actively tempting them with outright danger. Sometimes experimentation doesn't carry huge, immediate risks, but it can still feel daunting to some who worry only about short-term achievement rather than cognitive growth. A mix of willfully stretching oneself, acknowledging the real risks involved, making thoughtful decisions, and being able to absorb the consequences constitutes a healthy model for development.

## Opportunity Seeking Starts Early

So how can we foster opportunity seeking in our children? For decades, scholars have articulated a model for teaching children how to take forays into the unknown and deal with life's uncomfortable or risky moments. Attachment theory, as it is called, dates back to the seminal work of John Bowlby in the 1970s, and it continues to yield important research findings in child development. Attachment is often thought of as being synonymous with social bonding, but here the term has a more specific meaning. It refers to the *style* of relationship between a child and caregiver—how much a child can safely explore the world and go to the caregiver for comfort and support.

Think about a two-year-old going into a home he's never visited before with his parents. We'd expect him to rely on a parent as his secure base in this new environment. We wouldn't expect the toddler to just separate from the parent with no reservations—this would be unusual in such an unfamiliar situation. By the same token, we'd also hope that the toddler wouldn't be completely reticent—this would cut him off from the opportunity to explore. We would *hope* that he would feel safe enough to interact with the new people and surroundings while knowing his parents were there for support. Since any new situation can provide some discomfort—in this case, perhaps a dog barking unexpectedly—we'd anticipate that the toddler would turn to a parent for comfort. And the toddler would be happy to return to the parent's side.

A research method called the Strange Situation, developed by Dr. Mary Ainsworth in the 1970s, has helped us to assess attachment in the early years of life. Conducted in a laboratory, the Strange Situation follows a series of steps or episodes that reveal how a baby handles separation and reunion with a parent. Typically, parent and baby are brought into a room, and the parent is asked to let the baby explore on her own. Next, a stranger (the experimenter) comes into the room, talks to the parent, and talks to the baby. The parent is asked to slip out of the room without making a fuss. The baby thus encounters a separation, and the experimenter interacts positively with the baby. Then comes the reunion as the parent returns to the room and greets the baby. Another separation follows as the parent leaves *again* along with the experimenter, leaving the baby alone. The experimenter comes back in and plays with the baby. Finally, the parent returns, the experimenter leaves, and parent and child have their own "reunion."

The Strange Situation may seem somewhat contrived, but it was designed as a standardized way to simulate the flow of the familiar and unfamiliar in the everyday life of a baby. Researchers have devised an elaborate system for categorizing the parent-child dynamic as observed during the Strange Situation. "Secure attachment" is considered to be the desired dynamic; here, the baby explores a new environment (the unfamiliar laboratory room) without hesitation while the parent is present, the parent functioning as a "safe base." The baby will interact with the stranger with the parent present (again, more safe exploration); show some distress when the parent leaves (because the safe base is no longer present); and express happiness when the parent returns. On the other hand, "insecure attachment" is when a baby shows extreme distress even *with* the parent present and cannot be easily comforted when the parent returns. This means they don't have a secure base for adapting to new environments and will, in essence, be inhibited from seeking out new opportunities.

Decades of research have shown that the Strange Situation offers prediction of later adaptation across different developmental stages. In particular, attachment style helps determine *how children will navigate future challenges, cognitive as well as social.* It helps to predict which children will approach life knowing how to seek out new opportunities without taking frivolous or excessive risks, and without inhibitions that will override potential gains. Over time, securely attached children will serve as their own "secure base" for dealing with the unfamiliar and adapting to challenges; they will soothe *themselves* when necessary and not fear opportunities. By contrast, insecurely attached children may avoid new challenges altogether and not know how to deal with the unfamiliar. Or they may take risks indiscriminately without a real goal in mind.

A recent study published in the *Journal of School Psychology* confirmed the advantages of secure attachment—this time seen in how well children adapted to kindergarten. Researchers followed nearly 7,000 children from birth through childhood. Securely attached children were significantly better at adjusting to new situations in the classroom, showing an eagerness to learn and try new things. The securely attached kids had tools to push themselves to grow, knowing how to ease into unfamiliar situations and take on the unknown without that becoming daunting.

But, of course, let's remember that all children have different personalities. Some children are just more inhibited than others. The prominent developmental psychologist Jerome Kagan coined the phrase "behavioral inhibition" decades ago to describe a small percentage of toddlers who seem especially prone to shrinking back when faced with new situations, challenges, and people. Yet recent research suggests that even the most behaviorally inhibited children can be taught to get *past* their inhibitions. A research project using an adoption design (the Early Growth and Adoption Study) has teased apart how rearing conditions interact with biological risk for behavioral inhibition. A group of toddlers at high genetic risk for anxiety disorders—via a maternal history of anxiety—showed signs of behavioral inhibition *only when* their adoptive environments were characterized by low levels of parental warmth and responsiveness. Put another way, parental warmth can "override" the genetic tendency toward anxiety. Genes, while influential, don't determine everything.

> Parental warmth can "override" the genetic tendency toward anxiety.

## Being the Secure Base

What is the underlying factor that promotes secure attachment in babies, toddlers, and children? The consensus, based on decades of research, is *responsiveness to your child's emotions*. When a baby is distressed and its parent provides comfort, the baby learns that they can acknowledge negative emotions and *regulate* negativity. This is critical for healthy risk-taking and opportunity seeking. Kids need to develop, in the language of attachment theory, "inner working models" that guide emotional regulation and establish the notion that they can get distressed, because they will be soothed.

We might wonder about boundaries. What does it mean to be responsive as opposed to indulgent? Overreacting sends a message of fear, while underreacting conveys the pointlessness of expressing negative emotions—signaling that emotional regulation is not a priority. So how do you strike the right balance? Dr. Diane Benoit uses the example of crying in the first year of life. As she writes, attempting to soothe a baby is always a good thing in the first six months. "[L]etting a baby cry because it is 'good for their lung development' (as some parents argue clinically), because it will 'spoil' the baby or because the baby needs to find their own ways to self-soothe may not be advisable during the first six months of life." That said, during the second six months of life, when there is no substantial basis for crying (for example, injury, true emotional distress, illness), it makes sense to offer a little bit of soothing and then allow children the opportunity to regulate themselves. A little hug, a little kiss, a supportive word, and a dose of encouragement sends kids back on their way.

As kids get older, and the issues become more psychological, the same principles hold. Richard recalls one mother describing how her four-year-old daughter was inhibited socially and didn't want to go into her ballet class by herself. Mom thought she was helping her daughter by walking her into the room. A better strategy turned out to be encouraging her daughter—little by little—to make her *own* way into the dance class. Mom would point out a friendly face or get excited about the music being played or wave to the dance instructor. She acknowledged her daughter's shyness but didn't make too big a deal about it. In this way, she redirected attention toward the potential opportunity (fun in the class) rather than the negative aspect for her daughter (social discomfort). And by not entering the room, Mom could be an available safe haven *on the other side of the door* rather than an omnipresent safety blanket that could inhibit the daughter experiencing the payoff of exploring the new environment on her own.

Redirection toward the opportunity prevents children from becoming habitually fixated on minor setbacks they might experience. Claudia Hepburn is the executive director and cofounder of the Next 36, an exciting initiative in Canada that seeks to turn the country's top students into successful future business leaders and innovators. An entrepreneur and public policy specialist, Hepburn has a track record of leadership-building in innovative education programs. She suggests that parents respond *just enough* so that children can become empowered to regulate themselves during moments when they feel a little discomfort—for example, if a child cuts his knee:

> *Just stay calm and behave as if all is quite normal. They learn that it's usually only a matter of seconds and a couple of breaths before they recover. Children take a lot of cues from adults about what to get upset about and it's amazing how easily they will learn to endure these minor scratches that don't warrant more than a wipe and a Band-Aid before play can resume. Children then can get back to the action and don't learn that getting hurt brings them more of mum's attention, or worse, that mum teaches them to be afraid and cry when they see themselves bleed.*

Advice like this might seem easier said than done. Parents, especially those with infants and young children, are often tired, busy, and stressed. As a parent, you are not going to be nurturing and responsive every second of the day. But try to make a *balanced* response to distress the predominant experience for your child during those critical first years of life (and beyond).

## Early Confidence Boosters

Pediatrician Dr. Harvey Karp told us that developing a child's confidence plays a special role in encouraging secure attachment and healthy opportunity seeking: "Kids need to know that they can trust in themselves and confront new challenges and 'risks' in an appropriate and adaptive way. This gives them a sense that they can try new things." He provided us with three tips for parents seeking to help young children cultivate their confidence. First, you can encourage young children to take on small, attainable challenges—whether it's going down a slide that seems just a little too high (but in truth is just right for their age), using crafting scissors they aren't used to, or finding ways to help you prepare a meal. Children can get immediate reinforcement when they try something new and stick with it. When they climb up the steps to that higher slide, they learn to leave their comfort zone (literally and figuratively). After that first trip down the slide, they'll see that they *can* do it. And most important, getting back up there and sliding down again teaches them the mastery that comes from taking on a reasonable challenge.

Another tip from Dr. Karp is to let children choose from among lots of small challenges. This way, they learn that they don't have to take on every challenge that comes their way, but can focus on the ones that interest them most. A child who is shy on the playground may be rather daring in the kitchen, helping you cook. Other kids may have no interest in cooking but may want to help out with a baby sibling. Not every challenge is for every child, and it's helpful to send the message that they don't have to "prove themselves" every minute of the day. Plus, the more they gravitate to their interests, the more likely they will experience successes that build confidence.

Finally, Dr. Karp leverages his extensive experience working with toddlers to suggest a strategy he describes as "playing the boob" with them. Pretend you don't know how to do something "difficult" so they can jump in and show off their skills. Making this a little silly and fun is an easy way to engage them, and they will also get a sense of satisfaction that comes from doing something "hard to do."

## "Hands Off, Eyes On"

We've focused thus far on the early years; let's now consider how we might give older kids an ability to push beyond a comfort zone in a smart, "entrepreneurial" way. The real key is to know what *not* to do. If you've spent time around parents, you have probably witnessed a "helicopter parent" in action. Sure, "helicopter parent" is a bit of a caricature, but the reality is that some parents *clearly* push the boundaries of involvement. Some behaviors—like requesting a particular teacher in a particular school year or that certain children are or are not in their child's classroom—can seem innocuous. There very well might be a good reason to request a specific teacher. The problems start, however, when the "request" becomes an expectation or demand. In truth, parents shouldn't choose their child's teacher every year because that's not how the real world works. A child will not be able to select their teacher once they enter the higher grades, and certainly not when they get to high school and college. In addition, the parent is sending the child a message that they aren't capable of performing in a class unless the teacher is preselected for them. Children need to learn how to handle the twists and turns that come their way; they need to have experience dealing with all kinds of personalities.

"Snowplow parents," the latest incarnation of overinvolved parenting, don't just try to control a child's environment and experiences but *overtly eliminate perceived obstacles* in a child's path. Requesting that a specific child not be in your child's class is one thing; demanding to review and approve the class roster is quite another. It does not take a teacher long to figure out when a parent has gone from looking over their child's paper to writing it for them. Those amazing science projects that look like they took adult hands to accomplish *do* stand out to educators.

Think this phenomenon is limited to grade school? Carolyn O'Laughlin, director of residence life at Sarah Lawrence College, has written about snowplow parents infiltrating college campuses, in part via technologies such as Skype. She notes that the behaviors can extend far beyond the academic squabbles we might expect; parents now get involved in the minutiae of life, even intervening in "a dispute between roommates over a missing jar of peanut butter."

In Richard's experience as an educator, he's found that most parents are not this extreme (though, truth be told, a few stand out). That said, almost every parent has some of these instincts, and as the world becomes more competitive, it's understandable that parents want to give their kids an edge whenever they can. The thing to keep in mind, though, is recognizing the real edge you can give your child. Whether your child is an infant, a toddler, a child in sixth grade, or a college sophomore, your goal as a parent should be to support, nurture, and encourage without interceding much, allowing your child to develop his or her own competencies. If a child can't deal with a teacher that is not the preferred one, or classmates who prove themselves troublesome, or assignments in which an A is not a guarantee, how will they go out into the world and seek out complex challenges? How will they carve out the right opportunities and take calculated risks, like entrepreneurs? How will they ever make a big decision like giving up a stable teaching job to found a company when the timing seems favorable but success is not guaranteed?

By the same token, simply leaving a child to his or her own devices might promote some self-sufficiency, but it may also deprive them of the emotional support they need to navigate new demands. Recall that babies who don't have nurturing parents in the Strange Situation do not function optimally, and plenty of research suggests that they go on to become disruptive and unfocused in the classroom, or avoidant and passive. There is no question that children need nurturing, but the *right* kind of nurturing.

Startling data offered by sociologists Keith Robinson and Angel L. Harris reveal what healthy nurturing looks like. Conventional wisdom holds that *heavy* parental involvement in a child's education is a good thing, benefiting children and improving their academic performance. Robinson and Harris analyzed large surveys of American families extending from the 1980s to the 2000s. These surveys collected data on children's academic progress as well as indicators of parental involvement with their child's schoolwork. Robinson and Harris's sweeping conclusion was that "most parental behavior has no benefit on academic performance." Helping children with their homework did not improve children's actual academic progress. Perhaps more telling, frequent parental involvement (measured in a number of ways) often predicted *lower* academic performance.

That's not to suggest that parents have no role. According to Robinson and Harris, parents can support their children's education by sending a consistent message—starting as early as possible—that school is important in a child's life. Parents need to reinforce the value of school (and school activities) while leaving the actual work to the student. Robinson and Harris sum it up this way in a *New York Times* blog post: "What should parents do? They should set the stage and then leave it." This, again, is very much the model of secure attachment.

The basic tenet we propose is: "Hands off, eyes on." This idea applies across the ages and all the social contexts kids will find themselves in. It's okay to watch toddlers on the playground and keep your eyes on them in case they need you. But constantly intervening circumvents their opportunity to figure things out for themselves. It's okay to be around when they're doing homework, particularly if you are encouraging their academic achievement. But *inserting* yourself into their schoolwork undermines their development. Just like in the Strange Situation, leave the room, staying close enough to offer your emotional and practical support when needed.

## Failure Isn't an Option

Many parents are overprotective not because they want their children to succeed, but because they fear that they will fail. By contrast, many entrepreneurs believe that failure isn't an option—not because they're certain of their success, but because they don't define "failure" in the way that most people do. The only failure, entrepreneurs believe, lies in not trying, not stretching, not treating those risk-taking moments as opportunities for learning. Remember, entrepreneurs take risks in a calculated way. There is always that chance that an endeavor won't work out, but if it doesn't, entrepreneurs know that they will always take away something of value, just by pushing into the unknown. Therefore, "failure" is experience and direction for future behavior. In that sense, "failure" isn't an option because . . . it doesn't really exist.

Jen has essentially erased the word "failure" from her vocabulary. At work, she makes sure her employees treat "failure" as a learning experience; she notes that her company would not survive if her employees saw failures otherwise. When setbacks *do* happen, she sends an empowering message that you *can* change what you are doing, especially if you dig deep to figure out why something isn't working. She preaches it over and over: "What doesn't kill you makes you stronger." John Jacobs, cofounder and chief creative optimist of Life is good, likewise embraces mistakes for the learning they provide. "One of the biggest lessons we learned was

> When you try, you either succeed or you learn.

that when you try, you either succeed or you learn. These are both positive things. We learned to try to keep trying, to stay nimble enough to try new things, to make mistakes, to fall down, and to learn from all of that 'failure.' That's how you get smarter. If you fold your arms and tuck away and get defensive, it's not a good recipe to grow and develop."

Both Jen and John Jacobs also agree on a related principle: Every situation brings small successes, and kids need to learn how to recognize and embrace them. Sure, it's great to celebrate the big victories in a kid's life, but our children's days are filled with so many opportunities to affirm *little bits of progress* that eventually add up to bigger successes. Help your kid connect the dots and chart how little moments lead to bigger payoffs. At dinner, encourage your child to talk about how he felt more comfortable dribbling a basketball in today's practice than he did yesterday. Rather than reminding him that other kids are better dribblers and harping on this failing the second he leaves practice or a game, just reward this one little sign of progress. When he steals a pass during a game and dribbles full court for a game-winning layup, you can then make him aware of how many small successes led up to that big win.

This is *especially* important in relation to a child's progress in school. As a parent, you can best support academic development by encouraging children to focus on each small success they achieve. If he is struggling in math, focus on every little indicator that shows your child might be improving. Did he find one math problem easier than others? Did something in class make sense? Did he make more progress solving a tough algebra problem even if he didn't get the right answer? Parents can play a huge role in their child's life by helping them recognize and celebrate these moments. Keep in mind that the "celebration" is not throwing a party or buying a trophy or telling them they're becoming mathematical geniuses. We're talking about reinforcement—helping them see that their work is paying off and that *progress is being made.*

## A Growth Mindset: How Thinking Leads to Opportunity Seeking

Dr. Carol Dweck has performed decades of cutting-edge research on how parental language and behavior determine which "mindset" kids develop as they grow. She's found that some kids develop a "fixed" mindset, in which they pessimistically assume that their personal qualities are unalterable, and that negative experiences reveal their inherent limitations. Other kids develop a "growth" mindset, in which they assume that effort and dedication shape achievement. For these kids, failure doesn't represent the end of the road but a necessary bump that directs future effort.

Much has been written about the role of praise in determining which kind of mindset a child will develop. Dweck contends that praising kids for *their traits* reinforces the more pessimistic "fixed" mindset, while praising kids for *their efforts* reinforces an optimistic growth mindset. If your parents constantly tell you you're brilliant at science, and suddenly, your results—a series of C's—don't seem to bear that out, then you'll start to think that you're really not as smart as the other kids. If this is the case, you may become less motivated to improve the grade, because you may feel like you were simply mistaken about your abilities. This will be reinforced if your parents start panicking about your grades and indicating their disappointment. On the other hand, if you've been reinforced for your *hard work* in science over the years, you have received the message that applying yourself is the fundamental ingredient that yields good outcomes. Armed with this message, you can also greet adversity head-on, secure in the knowledge that changing how you direct your effort is likely to solve any problems.

That said, it's critical to recognize that Dweck's research isn't just about praise and how we should dole it out. It suggests how to instill that calculated opportunity seeking relished by many successful entrepreneurs. The growth mindset propels children (as well as adults) to embrace the unknown and take on challenges. They don't fear the unknown, because they know that any difficulties they encounter or failures they meet can be dealt with and are not a reflection on their identity or abilities. The way parents can instill a growth mindset is by *encouraging* children when they attempt activities that do not carry a guarantee of immediate success. Trying to reduce or eliminate obstacles—as "helicopter" and "snowplow" parents are characterized as doing—deprives children of the core experiences that help them develop a growth mindset.

Dweck's work also implies that parents should *limit criticism.* Criticism can be toxic to a child because it says, "Something about you—your fixed trait—isn't good enough." Some kids might respond to criticism by trying harder, but generally, hearing criticism becomes tiresome and sets up a pessimistic, fixed mindset. Every time a child slips or someone does better, she feels as though she is not measuring up, and over time, she concludes she just *can't do* the task in question. She throws in the towel. Rather than criticizing "mistakes," treat them as the targets for growth.

Consider the example of a kid who makes an error in a baseball game, causing his team to lose. It's not going to be easy for you, as a parent, to treat this as a learning moment right then and there. Your child will feel miserable, the kids on his team will be annoyed or angry, and other parents may not be pleasant about it—this is the real world. You may even have a reflex of: "C'mon, you gotta catch that!" But this is where you can really show your stuff as a parent. Be sympathetic without acting like the entire world has stopped spinning. Acknowledge that your kid is going to feel lousy for a while, but remind him that professional baseball players experience this, too—and when they are interviewed about it, they acknowledge the error but also indicate that they will be back at it tomorrow. When the next game starts, it really is a new game.

Parents should offer *realistic* support to help kids navigate the inevitable challenges they will face growing up. Praising effort and limiting criticism are certainly key elements, but the two bigger-picture takeaways are to encourage children's pursuits of challenges, and to focus proactively on what they can do *right now* to take on these challenges. When parents embrace difficult moments in their child's life, they bolster their child's psychological resources. Offering positive talk and support and strategizing about what was learned and what can be done moving forward help your child embrace the entrepreneurial idea that failures don't exist—only opportunities for growth.

## Will Today's Kids Be Tomorrow's Opportunity Seekers?

Much of the speculation on the downside of raising overprotected kids is based on the premise that they will not know how to function when they get out into the world. The reality is that we don't really have persuasive data one way or the other. We have a lot of impressions that kids are playing it too safe—but is that really what their futures hold?

Jen has hired many young people who are well equipped for the fast pace and challenges of her firm. There are always opportunities for these folks to "step up" to more and more responsibility—and there is room to "fail," grow, and progress. Jen also sees a few millennials that, despite all the hype, are not afraid to seek out the really big opportunities.

Jen recalls three such millennials, all of whom came into her office one day and told her that they were moving to Thailand to teach English to kids. At first, Jen was thinking that these kids were behaving rashly; they were on the fast track at her firm after all and were deciding to step off. But she ended up admiring and feeling proud of these kids. They had thought about what was right *for them*, and they were going to pursue that opportunity without obsessing about the potential negative consequences. They felt confident that this next phase of their lives was right for them and that they would grow from it. They weren't just seeking out something dramatic or doing something risky for the sake of it. They were thoughtful, strategic opportunity seekers. What more could we want for our children?

# 5

||||||||||||||||||||

# Doers

Golnar Khosrowshahi is founder and president of Reservoir Media Management, an independent music publisher based in New York City and Toronto. Always highly competitive and notoriously unpredictable, music publishing has become an even tougher business as of late, thanks to the Internet. Whereas once consumers bought an entire album from a limited number of retail outlets, they can now buy individual songs online, choosing from suppliers the world over. Prices have declined, and with them, revenue for music publishers. Still, success is possible. Since 2007, Reservoir has amassed a diverse catalog of more than 30,000 songs, including works by artists such as Beyoncé, Drake, Tim McGraw, and Madonna. Reservoir holds rights to the *America's Got Talent* theme song and placed songs by Usher and 50 Cent in the movie *The Hangover*. Reservoir has demonstrated a unique ability to seek out opportunities at a time when many independent music publishers are finding it hard just to stay in business.

We approached Khosrowshahi for an interview because we knew she regularly encounters young people seeking to get into the music business. We asked her about the kids she met, and what she thought the biggest issues were facing parents today. Khosrowshahi did not hesitate: "I believe that one of the biggest challenges we face as parents is that our children have every ingredient to grow up to be entitled, and this sense of entitlement could be the downfall of this generation." Many people share Khosrowshahi's view. In numerous blogs and articles, cultural observers argue that members of the rising generation are growing up thinking they don't have to work hard (or at all) to get what they want. If we were to craft a caricature of youth today, they might possess the following attitudes:

» "I am special and should be treated as such at all times."

» "Gifts are not something to be cherished; I assume they're coming to me."

» "I shouldn't have to wait to get things I want; I should get what I want when I want it."

» "Teachers should recognize my brilliance and treat me as gifted. I should never see anything but an A on my report card."

» "I should get accepted into the college of my choice."

» "Upon graduation, my dream job should be waiting for me and it should involve people doing things for me and not the other way around."

Is this sketch accurate? It can be in some cases. If you spend any time working with youth as an educator or employer, you are guaranteed to encounter elements of this thinking in *certain* people. Richard has met his share of entitled kids while interacting with college students. Once, a student stormed into his office, demanding that his grade of C be changed to an A. The student didn't question why he received a C; he insisted he receive an A without further discussion. Richard pushed back, arguing that the student's work throughout the semester consistently fell in the C range.

"That doesn't matter," the student countered. "I know the material perfectly and should be rewarded for that."

"So why did you only get a 75 on your final exam?"

"The exam was flawed. It didn't test what I knew."

In the spirit of open discussion, Rende acknowledged that the test could be flawed, but if it was, why had other students received higher grades? With some even getting a perfect score? "Here's my dilemma," Richard said. "If a 75 warrants an A, what kind of grade should the students who received a 100 get for the course?"

That ended the conversation.

To be fair, it *is* good for young people to know how to

advocate for themselves. It is certainly legitimate for a student to pose factual questions about whether an exam is graded correctly. The line gets crossed when a student departs from the factual and either lobs vague accusations about an instructor's careless grading or presumes that they inherently deserve a particular grade. Happily, Richard has encountered plenty of students who don't cross that line; they are diligent in their work and accept responsibility for their performance. One student was close to failing even though he was being tutored. He spent time working with Richard to change how he was approaching the course material and continued to try new study methods. Thanks to his consistent efforts, he managed a solid B+ on his final exam. More than the grade, this student achieved a deep satisfaction that comes from working hard to achieve meaningful results. This is by far the more typical story in Richard's experience.

Still, Khosrowshahi and others who regularly observe the behavior of young people in their earliest work experiences may be on to something when observing the increased entitlement of today's youth. It's not that young people don't want to work hard. Rather, it's more the idea that they don't necessarily want to work hard *at certain tasks that they perceive to be menial,* and they anticipate being rewarded for things they haven't yet accomplished. Anecdotally, some kids seem to believe that they shouldn't have to start at an entry-level position and take on low-level grunt work—what we call "dirty jobs." They feel they should be recognized for their high level of abilities and leapfrog right to the top. For entrepreneurs like Khosrowshahi, this "entitled" mindset isn't just troubling for its arrogance but because it prevents kids from achieving success. In any field, you need to learn as much as you can about the basic work that is done before you can perform at higher levels. The only way to gain true expertise is to do things yourself and immerse yourself in the details. "Dirty jobs" aren't a form of exploitative hazing delivered by older workers; rather, these jobs are an essential starting point on the path to competence, proficiency, and eventually mastery. And in our experience we have observed that top-level people in many fields still take on "dirty jobs" on a daily basis as a necessary step for them to strive for success.

## Generation Me Versus Generation We?

Social scientists disagree about whether today's youth feel and act more entitled than previous generations. In her paper "The Evidence for Generation Me and Against Generation We," published in *Emerging Adulthood*, Dr. Jean Twenge analyzed a number of studies, finding strong evidence for a rise in a sense of entitlement. As she acknowledges, most studies have not measured "entitlement," but a number of related constructs such as narcissism and self-esteem. Narcissism is defined as "having a very positive, inflated view of the self." It's the word "inflated" that connects narcissism with entitlement. Narcissism is measured by a questionnaire kids fill out that asks about a wide range of self-perceptions that, taken together, represent the extent to which someone views himself or herself in a narcissistic manner. Twenge cites surveys of college students, gathered at regular intervals between 1980 and 2009, which show a steady increase in narcissism over time—with students in 2009 boasting the highest levels of narcissism. While these results are statistically significant, the magnitude of the change is still somewhat modest.

Twenge further suggests that levels of self-esteem have been increasing in samples of children as well, to the point where children now harbor artificially inflated self-concepts. Studies of high school students show that they are endorsing increasingly positive views of themselves. As Twenge points out, these boosts in self-perception do not parallel rises in achievement and effort. While samples of college students (with data collected between 1966 and 2010) report higher perceptions of their academic drive, their test scores haven't been going up, and, in fact, the amount of time students spend studying has been declining. Increasing numbers of America's youth appear to be seeing themselves in an inaccurately positive light.

Dr. Jeffrey Jensen Arnett was not convinced by Twenge's approach and analyses. Responding in *Emerging Adulthood*, he argued that the questionnaires in Twenge's narcissism studies did not reflect a particularly valid trait, and that some of the attributes captured were actually positive. Further, Arnett argues, Twenge was wrong to rely so much on college students, who hardly represent all youth. A number of papers did *not* find increased narcissism and related traits in recent generations.

Parents benefit from the dialogue that goes on in academic

journals such as *Emerging Adulthood*. Still, as we think about parenting strategies, we so often want research findings that reflect a consensus. The truth is that research often chases societal trends. As the healthy, academic debate between Twenge and Arnett reveals, research doesn't perfectly assess the constructs we discuss in the popular press. The types of data that are available can be interpreted in multiple ways, leading to divergent scholarly opinions. It's not easy to come away with a clear-cut, takeaway message—much as we might want to.

In the case of entitlement, though, it may not be *necessary* to come to a clear conclusion. Entrepreneurs and educators are observing troubling patterns in our children's behavior. Further, they're spotting these patterns at key, transitional moments in our children's lives—when they're embarking on careers and getting their first taste of "the real world." Whether a kid *comes across* as entitled can make the difference between a job offer and no callback, or between a coveted slot in graduate school and a rejection letter. An entrepreneur like Khosrowshahi running a high-profile music business is flooded with résumés. The applicants that stand out don't just have high grades or talent. They show diligence and grit—a willingness to get their hands dirty and outwork the competition. As Khosrowshahi puts it, she wants young people who are "self-sufficient and responsible for themselves. They need to be *doers*."

## Chores: Good News and Bad News

One way to cultivate self-sufficiency and responsibility seems obvious, right? Give children chores. Prevailing wisdom holds that kids learn a sense of responsibility by performing tasks around the house with regularity. Ultimately, kids learn that they have to take care of themselves; they understand that other people are not going to handle everything for them and clean up their messes. They recognize that we *all* must deal with the routine, mundane drudgery of life. Most important, they discover that doing grunt work *now* leads to desirable outcomes over the long term.

A few longitudinal studies illustrate the importance of performing chores during childhood. The first is a long-term study of 200 Harvard male undergraduates that began in the late 1930s. Researchers found that involvement in chores in early childhood was the most powerful predictor of positive psychological adjustment late in life. In the second study, researchers found that participating in chores early in life was strongly associated with personal and academic success twenty years later.

Because both of these studies involved analyses of data collected over decades, they provide strong evidence that chores help. But these researchers looked at a very select group of individuals born sometime between the 1930s and the 1960s. What about kids today? One research effort that has received widespread attention is a multidisciplinary examination of middle-class families in Los Angeles conducted by UCLA's Center on Everyday

Lives of Families (CELF). Investigators have used a variety of methods to study everyday life, including questionnaires, videotaping, and direct recordings of real-time observations by research staff while in participants' homes. The study's findings deliver some bad news about children and chores.

In one of their reports, published in 2009, CELF researchers looked at thirty middle-class, dual-earner families in Los Angeles and found that children spent "surprisingly little time helping around the house." Meanwhile, children in these families reported spending *more* time on household tasks than they really were. Since chores weren't a regular, recurring part of children's lives, they seemed like an intrusion to these kids, not something accepted as worthwhile or valuable. So is this strong evidence of entitlement? Not necessarily—we should be careful not to generalize about an entire generation based on a study that covered only a very small number of families. Still, the methods of data collection deployed by CELF researchers yield a detailed picture of the lives of these families. We would be remiss not to take notice.

In some cases, it's understandable that children would regard chores as burdensome and excessive—partly because they are cast in that light, and partly if the load exceeds what a child is capable of doing. Taking on more responsibility doesn't *inherently* translate into positive outcomes for youth. If *some* chores are good, it doesn't follow that piling on more and more of them is even better. Our challenge as parents, therefore, would seem to be to find the right balance between chores and leisure in a child's life that would allow them to reap developmental benefits.

One familiar technique you might think to try is giving your children an allowance. On the surface, an allowance would seem to make sense; it provides a regular incentive for a child, as well as an immediate reinforcement once the work is performed. Yet the CELF research found that allowance is *not* an effective motivator to get kids to do chores. Once a child is offered compensation for a task, it's no longer a chore: It's a job. You learn that if you do your job properly, you get paid. If you do a lousy job, maybe you don't get paid. All this is well and good, but the payment itself is just an *external* reward. It would be far stronger if we could offer kids *internal* rewards—like positive feelings that spur kids to do more than the bare minimum and to invest themselves emotionally in their work.

When Jen brings a new person into her firm, she isn't looking for someone who's just going to perform the duties listed in the job description—she's looking for someone who is going to go *beyond* that and proactively take on new responsibilities or initiatives.

In a complex business like a PR firm, it may not even be clear, on a given day and at a given moment, what tasks need to be accomplished. Part of the job may be figuring out what *needs* to happen. People who adhere strictly to their job description probably won't flourish under these conditions, or remain in the job very long. Simply sticking to what you are "getting paid to do" can certainly be beneficial in some lines of work, but it's not a guiding principle for the entrepreneurial vision of success.

# Making Kids Do Their Chores?

Forget about allowances—what if we simply *make* kids do chores? Again, this approach might seem to make sense. Many parents today didn't receive allowances as children; they were simply told what to do and when to do it. Being forced to do chores reinforces the stature of parents as authority figures, and it also infuses a work ethic in kids. Yet there are hidden drawbacks to this. Making chores mandatory doesn't allow kids to learn other lessons associated with household tasks, such as being self-sufficient. Rather, it encourages compliance. Now, compliance isn't the worst thing in the world; kids really do need to listen to their parents. Still, if compliance is *all* that spurs kids to perform chores, they're hardly learning how to develop their own drive and initiative.

Indeed, young children often do not comply immediately with a strict edict, especially when such commands become a dominant mode of communication. Note here we are drawing a distinction between those times when a parent needs to issue a directive (say, when a child is approaching a hot oven) and the consistent use of harsh methods. Inevitably, the parent *escalates* the demand (usually speaking louder and angrier), prompting the child to respond similarly. You might have seen this dynamic unfold on occasions when you have taken a strict stance. How effective is it *really* when you dictate your requests, yelling and screaming when your child doesn't jump to attention? It's pretty clear that simply *demanding* that children perform chores won't nurture them into becoming doers. Sometimes they will become compliant, responding to external requests. But more frequently the nagging and yelling will only make them angry, and the chores will go uncompleted.

## Making Chores Internally Rewarding

We all know that chores aren't fun. They're "have to do" activities rather than "want to do." An intriguing paper by Dr. Michael Inzlicht and colleagues explored the cognitive science behind people's tendencies to drift from what they "have to do" in favor of what they "want to do." Inzlicht theorizes that motivation profoundly influences cognitive functioning and the allocation of mental resources. Individuals muster willpower and self-control when they can connect their behavior with an *internalized* desirable outcome (as opposed to a desirable outcome that comes about from an external source). For instance, you can undermine your interest in going to the gym later today (rather than going out for a fun meal) by exclusively referencing the advice dispensed by an outside authority, such as a doctor or nutritionist. What would work better is to remind yourself that making a healthy choice will have a tangible influence on your health and contribute to weight management. Much of the time, we need a very strong, internal motivator to prompt us to do grunt work we would rather not perform.

We can apply this study to the task of getting kids to do chores and, more broadly, to the goal of helping kids become doers. While chores are inherently unpleasant, reinforcing this notion (by nagging, bartering, or bribing) *reduces* rather than increases the likelihood that kids will allocate the mental resources necessary to perform chores. Demanding and nagging simply program into kids the notion that chores are low-motivation tasks—work that *clearly* is "have to do" rather than "want to do." External rewards, whether it's praise or payment, also get processed cognitively as signals that chores are not high-motivation tasks.

So should we spare chores altogether? Not at all. As parents, one strategy is to take something that is not fun ("have to") and turning it, as much as possible, into something that *is* fun ("want to"). Television shows and songs do this when they portray kids performing chores while singing and dancing. Those fun little parenting tips that suggest turning *chore time* into *playtime* are, in fact, supported by the latest thinking in cognitive science. If you have a toddler or a young child, invite them to join you in straightening up or setting the table while you sing and laugh; you'll find it's a much more effective invitation than a nag or command. If you put on some music and dance around a little as you work, you can further signal that completing household tasks is not a dreary experience to be avoided.

Lightening the mood is certainly a good thing. That said, an even more influential approach would be to do chores *together*. You will give your child a social reason to want to join in and model for them that taking care of things isn't inherently all doldrums. A communal sense of caretaking can be conveyed this way. And whether you are folding laundry or washing the car, you and your child can enjoy some uninterrupted time when they can recount what's happening in their lives, knowing that you are paying close attention. Chores can become part of the social fabric of family time.

Of course, it's also good to have kids do some chores on their own. When young children complete chores, they affirm to themselves that they are *competent*. This constitutes another type of internal motivation—as well as a sense of self that differs substantially from the entitled thinking that says, "I am special and someone should always do things for me." It is internally rewarding to take care of oneself and feel independent—tasks that allow us to feel this way naturally become "want to" activities. Some parents find that a chore board works well, giving kids a chance to track what they have to do and what they've already accomplished. Just be sure that you aren't handing off too onerous a load. Toddlers may be delighted and able to sort socks, but asking them to fold shirts perfectly will probably frustrate them— and you. You know your child better than anyone else. Just think of what they can do and what they *like* to do. Richard recalls that when his daughter was a toddler, she liked how napkins were folded in restaurants. When the family had dinner guests, his daughter enjoyed helping set the table, since she got to fold napkins in creative ways. Turn your kid loose and let them show off their blossoming skills. They'll start to feel more and more effective—and they'll be more motivated to do what you ask them to.

Be mindful not to overpraise once a chore is completed; this type of external reward can undermine the more powerful internal ones, and it also implicitly frames the chore as something inherently unpleasant. Think about things you can say (adopting a cheerful tone of voice) that will nudge kids to reinforce for *themselves* the benefits that a chore yielded. As an example, you might ask your child, "How do you feel now that you've put all your toys away?" In general, try not to emphasize drudgery when you talk about chores. Instead, affirm that some elements of chores can *directly benefit* the child. Emphasize to a toddler that putting a few toys away helps ensure that they won't get broken accidentally. When talking to a tween or teen, point out that putting clothes away helps them continue to look good. Try to frame household chores in a positive light. Children are always observing the emotions of their parents; if you are as cheerful as possible about the responsibilities you shoulder, they will likely develop a similar perspective.

## Learning to Work by Watching and Doing

Many entrepreneurs we spoke with recalled spending time with their parents while they were at work. As young children, they got the chance to see their parents doing all kinds of tasks, and it helped them understand how taking on small jobs enabled completion of a bigger job. Golnar Khosrowshahi of Reservoir Media Management recalls: "My brother and I spent our weekends at the office/factory with our parents on Saturdays, as they worked six days a week. We spent a good amount of time with various people who worked there. We learned a great deal from the administrative staff—how to be organized, how to communicate, how to write a letter. Our favorite game growing up was 'office' where we were colleagues and constantly dealing with emergencies such as goods not being delivered."

Nick Sarillo, founder and CEO of two Chicago-area restaurants and author of the book *A Slice of the Pie: How to Build a Big Little Business*, had many such influential experiences growing up. From the age of ten, Sarillo spent summers working with his dad's construction company and aluminum siding business. He learned that there were lots of unglamorous things that had to be done in order to run a business well. "He would have me start the day by picking up scrap metal and throwing it away. He taught me how to carry ladders so I could move things around with him. It's not like he was driving me hard; I would work for an hour and then rest and sit next to him for an hour. I would go in the middle of the day and take a nap in the front seat of the truck."

Later, Sarillo worked at his dad's beef stand, doing anything from sweeping the floor to taking sandwiches to others. Over time, Sarillo perceived how his dad's livelihood depended on getting all these miscellaneous jobs done. Sarillo received no external compensation and no one was saying that he *had* to work; the work was just there and it had to be done. "This is where I got this mindset of 'I can do anything,'" Sarillo reflects. "'Can't' wasn't really in our vocabulary. We were going to work hard to get where we needed to go because we need to do whatever we need to do. Working hard was the only way to get there."

If your child spends time in the workplace with you, she'll learn that there is nothing degrading about menial tasks, and that even distinguished, highly paid professional workers commonly attend to them in the course of their jobs rather than expecting someone else to do them. Richard recalls the first academic conference he went to as a graduate student; he went early to secure a good seat for a lecture delivered by a prominent researcher and psychiatrist. When he got to the room fifteen minutes before the talk, he saw the researcher picking up debris from the floor and straightening out chairs. If Richard had brought his daughter with him, she would have discovered first-hand that successful people don't think it's "beneath them" to take care of mundane chores. On the contrary, an embrace of dirty jobs is part and parcel of a success mindset.

Not every parent can bring their kids to work with them. If this is the case for you, let your child observe you if you ever bring work home. Share with her the many things you need to do to make progress. Find ways to have her pitch in. Again, as was the case with chores, you'll want to be sure to assign her tasks that she can complete on her own. Get creative about how to involve your child. Richard had his young daughter help format and operate his PowerPoint presentation when he gave talks at professional conferences. These were things she enjoyed doing, and they gave her an opportunity to feel a sense of competence and accomplishment in a real-world context.

## Those First Early Jobs:
## Meaning Versus Money

Nick Sarillo not only believes in the impact work can have on a young person; he has instituted a unique work program at his Chicago restaurant, bringing inexperienced teens into the business and providing them with training that helps them understand the value of "dirty jobs." The program is carefully designed to instill a sense of responsibility and independence. For instance, when employees start at Nick's, they receive a folder with their training materials that they have to keep track of—a manager won't do it for them. Once they're on the job, employees have to proactively elect to train in new skills rather than being assigned to do so. Since raises are pegged to further training, employees determine for themselves how much effort they want to put in and how much money they will make. "We're holding them accountable to their own development and performance," Sarillo explains.

Sarillo knows that this sense of accountability helps spark internal motivation not just in kids, but in young adults, too; they are able to see work as something *they* choose and manage. Nick supports his young workers by clearly communicating that he and every other employee believe in them and think that they are important and valuable. Through such efforts, activities such as cleaning the floors and chopping vegetables become "want to do" activities. Kids take pride in their work and see it as the basis for later achievements. As time passes, they develop their skills, take on new responsibilities, and internalize personal lessons they've learned.

During the early teen years, involvement in paid or volunteer jobs can begin to cultivate a sense of work's desirability by helping kids perceive the tangible *products* of work. Josh Baron and Rob Lachenauer, writing in the *Harvard Business Review* blog, have strongly endorsed the idea of summer jobs for kids. They suggest that these early work experiences encourage discipline, foster a grounded attitude, and instill a notion that every job must be done well. "Kids that have jobs—even part-time or volunteer jobs—are more successful, both personally and professionally."

Not everyone agrees that a summer job is a ticket to success—and, in fact, some suggest it may impede today's youth. A working paper by Drs. Christopher Ruhm and Charles Baum, published in the *National Bureau of Economic Research*, examined longitudinal data collected on two groups of youth. One group of more than 12,000 people between fourteen and twenty-one years of age began participating in the study in 1979; a second group of about 9,000 youth between the ages of twelve and sixteen started the survey in 1997. Both groups continued to provide data into their adult years. Thanks to this research design, researchers can compare two "cohorts" separated by twenty years. In the older generation, researchers observed clear and long-lasting advantages to having a summer job; kids who had held summer jobs reported income (in their later twenties) that was more than eight times higher than those who didn't have summer jobs as teens. This benefit, however, was much slighter for the 1997 cohort, leading some to suggest that summer work now offers a more limited benefit.

Survey data such as this offers an incomplete picture. Whether today's youth wind up making more money later on thanks to their teenage jobs, they will still develop a sense of involvement, responsibility, and accomplishment that will serve them throughout their careers. Nick Sarillo's teens aren't just working to make some money or showing up to do what they are told. Being part of Sarillo's team provides them with *meaningful* work experiences that impact their lives.

Sure, the financial benefits of summer work are important. But the *real* benefits emerge when work experiences connect with something inside the child. Nonpaying internships and volunteer opportunities can also enable kids to pursue new interests and tackle unglamorous tasks. In some cases, volunteer positions are ideal because they usually require that kids take on "whatever needs to get done" rather than very prescribed job responsibilities. Anything children can do to connect with internal motivations in the "real world" will prove beneficial, motivating them to want to work more.

Even just looking for a position, whether volunteer or paid, can benefit kids, helping them become more attuned to seizing opportunities as they arise. When Richard was in college, he helped pay his tuition by participating in a mandatory work-study program during both the summer and the school year. His university had a medical school, and during his sophomore year, he found a job in the business office of the genetics department. For some kids, this would have been an interesting job opportunity, but Richard was not interested in business, and working through the complex invoices seemed unappealing. One day after work, he decided to take a walk around the medical school. He saw a poster advertising a work-study opportunity in the department of neuroanatomy as a research assistant. He pounced on that chance, landed the job, and within weeks was learning all kinds of research methods. That job became so important to him that he began to skip class just to put in extra time, without getting paid. Why sit in a lecture hall and see pictures of the brain flashed on the screen when you can actually dissect one yourself?

The full benefits of immersing teens in "the real world" are unpredictable, and they sometimes don't reveal themselves until well into adulthood. Jen had her share of "teen" jobs—bagging groceries, for instance, or working in the customer service department of an electronics store. Later on, she held a number of internships in law firms, market research firms, and public relations firms. Looking back on all these experiences, she realizes that she had put in an extraordinary amount of time learning how to behave in an office environment long before she started "working" in them. In all, she had accumulated two full years of collective experience before she even hit her first day of full-time work. That kind of seasoning gave her a running head start in her career. Did it help her make more money during the course of her career? It's hard to say. But dollars and cents don't come close to telling the whole story.

## "Doing" in School

We've talked about the home and the workplace. The other important place where children learn to become conscientious and industrious "doers" is at school. Even in the earliest years, school enables children to demonstrate a degree of independence and self-sufficiency. For instance, preschoolers must be capable of getting themselves to and from the classroom once they are dropped off at the designated spot. During the seemingly innocuous routine of dropping off and picking up a toddler, parents have a valuable opportunity to encourage their children to behave independently and gain confidence in their abilities.

Jen had an epiphany when her daughter was just two years old. She calls it her "Montessori Moment." Jen brought her daughter to her first day at preschool, and the teachers were greeting parents for the first time. At the end of the session, one of the teachers stood up and said, "Parents, please don't be insulted, but you must stop putting on their shoes for them and carrying them down the stairs at pickup. At school they do these things on their own." Jen realized how she had been unwittingly inhibiting her daughter's own development up to that point. By never allowing her daughter to put her shoes on for herself or walk down the stairs alone, Jen had been depriving her of the opportunity to experience a moment of independence and self-sufficiency. Like Jen, many parents think they are helping their children by performing small, everyday tasks for them. Even at very young ages, though, children are capable of doing on their own. Allowing them to figure out a task gives them a chance to learn and grow.

At preschool, toddlers may share in doing classroom "jobs," rotating their responsibilities on a weekly basis. This is a very nice tradition, one that can continue well into the school years. In conversations Richard has had, some parents have questioned this practice. A few have claimed that the kids shouldn't be doing the jobs that people at a school get paid to do. That thinking misses the point. Classrooms are the children's "homes" while they are at school. In the classroom, kids develop a sense of responsibility and pride in doing their jobs. They know how to keep track of what "job" they will have for the week and can do that "job" without prompting by the teacher. They become doers, as they begin to cultivate industriousness (the tendency to work hard to achieve a goal) during the childhood years.

## Schoolwork

As kids get older, the most important "work" they perform in school is, of course, the business of learning. Academic work offers children extraordinary opportunities to develop a strong work ethic. A recent scholarly review confirmed that conscientiousness and industriousness begin to emerge in the early school years, no doubt influenced by the increasing autonomy that the school setting enables. Here parents can be profoundly influential or, alternately, detrimental. We've discussed how helicopter and snowplow parenting undermine a child's ability to acquire a growth mindset and take appropriate risks. These parental behaviors can also undermine the development of strong work habits. Children need to do most (if not all) of their school projects by themselves. Doing it for them—and hoping to secure good grades for them in the process—doesn't promote their emerging sense of mastery, nor does it encourage them to stick with tasks and manage themselves responsibly.

Volumes have been written about the critical importance of "intrinsic motivation" throughout the formal school years. Such motivation is the essence of what children need at school to assure their immediate and later academic successes. We're not talking about getting the highest grades per se, but rather cultivating and accruing all the benefits of working hard. As just one example, Drs. Rebecca Shiner and Ann Masten have shown that the emerging motivation to master tasks during childhood predicts the tendency to work hard and thrive at challenges at age thirty. The endgame, in other words, isn't your child's grade on their science project in the sixth grade; it's whether or not they are motivated to do that project and put in their best effort. That only comes with actually doing the work.

So how might parents try to cultivate "mastery motivation" (a child's internal drive to become good at something—think "mastering" a task) and "intrinsic motivation" (internal desire rather than reliance on external reward) at school? It comes down to *attitude*. Kids need to understand your expectations about their effort and involvement with school; they should get the message that putting in the time to do their best at schoolwork is valued and a priority for them. They should appreciate that immersing themselves in the work matters more than the result, so there is no reason why you would do any of their work for them.

Distractions should be kept to a minimum when kids are doing their schoolwork. Encourage kids to get their work done and *then* enjoy other interests and activities. They should also have a daily schedule that encourages good work habits. It's worth discussing with your kids how they can plan out their days to get homework done; that way, they start to see the importance of structuring time responsibly. In all of these ways, a parent isn't doing the work *for* the child but rather creating a physical, emotional, and cognitive context that sets the foundation for the type of effort that will inspire the motivation to master tasks.

And that's a key point. A certain amount of effort and discipline is required to "turn on" children's desire to do for themselves. The internal motivation comes from doing and finding out that accomplishing something feels good. Subject matter can become a lot more interesting when effort is applied well. An analogy is exercise. Some of us may dread the idea of going for a run or hitting the gym. But once we start doing it—once our body and our mind experience the pleasure that comes from that effort—we become much more motivated to re-create that feeling. There is no shortcut. No one can do it for you. You have to devote yourself to it, and once you get started, the motivation grows. It's the same for kids with schoolwork.

## Getting Beyond Grades

Taking an interest in your child's schoolwork—*not their grades, but the content*—sends the strongest message of all. So much attention is paid to grades, at every level of education, these days that they can overshadow most other matters, for both parents and kids. On one level, this emphasis is understandable and even laudable. Grades are a definable metric at a time when schools across the country are focused on testing and scores. And grades do send signals about current mastery. But when grades override an appreciation of the underlying process of learning, particularly a child's level of engagement and their work habits, then problems arise.

Think about the questions you ask your child after school. Do your most urgent queries concern grades handed out or preparation for upcoming exams? It's important to keep tabs on performance, but having daily conversations about interesting things learned in school (admittedly, a somewhat retro idea) is more effective than you might think. It lets your children know that you are aware of their hard work and that you value it. And it also lets you identify topics that generate interest and excitement in your child. If your child finds history interesting, encourage him to talk about what he is learning. Observing his sparks of interest and fanning those flames go a long way toward reinforcing his own curiosity, excitement, and emerging "mastery motivation."

Rather than doing your children's homework for them, talk more broadly with them about the *content* of that homework. Kids are much more curious about the world than we often realize. They *like* conversations that stimulate their curiosity, and they are less thrilled with being "talked to" or "grilled" to see how much they are learning. You might be pleasantly surprised to find how eloquently your child talks about a math problem if you give him the chance to discuss it conversationally. Whether your child is having an easy or a hard time in math, ask him to tell you what material he is learning and what it means to him. If he is having trouble, encourage him to articulate what is confusing to him. Don't do this to help him get the right answer on his homework. It's not about the grade. It's about sparking interest and passion for the material that *in turn* will lead to better grades and deeper learning.

Grades serve to cue parents into what's working and what isn't. A low grade should spur you to think about what to do next to help your child progress. Talk to your child and partner with her teacher. Shift control to your child, encouraging *her* to identify and try new strategies. Reinforce the importance of taking on challenges even if the outcome isn't exactly ideal. And if your child is racking up A's, help her identify what's going right and what she's doing to achieve them. Explicitly tying her grade to her work habits anticipates what you might say in the future if her schoolwork gets tougher and she finds an "A" harder to come by.

> Grades serve to cue parents into what's working and what isn't.

What you *shouldn't* do is tie performance to a reward. Paying for grades runs contrary to decades of research in developmental science and education on the importance of intrinsic motivation. Most of the recent research on paying for grades suggests that it produces very modest success at best, and typically little impact at all. Underperforming schools have experimented with paying for grades on a large scale, and as the research of Harvard's Dr. Roland Fryer has shown, the actual impact on grades is quite minimal (though some effects accrue in terms of increased effort).

## Doing for Themselves Out in the World

If we want to counter whatever trends may exist that promote entitlement in today's kids—and if we desire, instead, to see our kids grow up with a strong work ethic and a drive to succeed—then there's no substitute for helping our children cultivate positive attitudes about being doers. Let's get them excited to work hard and make sacrifices today toward larger goals. Let's help them to see just how satisfying a job can be, even if it involves something mundane such as sweeping the floors, cleaning off tables, or yes, making pizza. And let's make sure that they transition into doing for themselves when the time comes rather than relying on us, as parents, to do for them.

Jen has seen evidence that some kids are *not* ready for the real world. She's had parents of *twenty-four-year-olds* call her to ask if their sons or daughters could get an interview to work in her firm. That's not really screaming volumes about the prospective applicant's tendency to be a doer. Similarly, Suzanne Cohon, who owns the prominent ASC Public Relations firm in Toronto, looks for that kind of young person who is self-motivated and is ready to do. She reflects on her own experiences growing up as one of four children. It was assumed that each child would have a certain degree of self-sufficiency and initiative. She recalls how she took her own mini-tour of campuses—*completely on her own*—when she was applying to colleges. She had to figure out how to get there and navigate the experience herself. While it's important that parents support their children as they consider where they are going to school, Cohon's experiences—which resonate with Jen, who also made her own way to visit schools when she was looking into colleges—remind us that we have to be thoughtful about how we let our kids assume their own responsibility for transitioning into independence. Richard has heard many a dean of admissions for a college say that same thing to parents: Stop using the word "we" when you are talking about your child's college application process. You and your child are not applying—your child is the only one applying to the school. He should be doing his own application, and yes, as much as possible, having a good amount of independent time when he is visiting a campus and trying to learn about what it would be like to attend that school.

It can be hard for parents who want to make sure that their child is as successful as possible getting into the best college they can. Supporting him is one thing. Doing for him is another. Your child needs to be the doer. Colleges can tell pretty easily if you, or your child, wrote the essay that is part of the application. Let him do it himself. Being a doer will not only pay off for him in the short term in many ways, but will also prove to be invaluable later in life.

> Your child needs to be the doer.

# PEOPLE SKILLS

When Pippa Lord was a college student in Australia with interests in culture, fashion, and photography, she found herself making connections with professionals in these areas. Through this process she landed an attractive opportunity to work as a publicist before she even finished college. This work led in short order to another, much larger opportunity: a six-week internship in New York City with her favorite fashion magazines, *V* and *V Man*. It was Lord's first trip to the United States, and scarcely had she arrived when she struck gold again: She was offered a paying job as the photo and bookings editor of both magazines, working with Karl Lagerfeld and Hedi Slimane, her fashion idols.

New York fashion magazines certainly do not dole out internships and place young people in critically important positions without first *carefully scrutinizing* their abilities. But Lord recalls that she had certain strengths, in addition to her basic business intelligence, that she found quite powerful and influential: interpersonal skills. "I believe that simply having good people skills was a critical reason I got such amazing opportunities in my early twenties. I was nice. I was happy. I worked hard. I was pleasant and fun. I knew how to work with people. I realized that people like to be around people they like, especially in the workplace, and they feel good about trusting others to take on big responsibilities."

Lord continued to hone her "people" or social skills along with her many other talents. Good thing, because after five years at *V*, her next job as photo director at *Elle* magazine required them in spades. As Lord discovered, it's not easy to navigate the personalities and delicate egos involved in a high-profile photo shoot. But Lord thrived in the job. After three years at *Elle*, she took an entrepreneurial step in her career and founded the chic lifestyle website Sous Style, which offers a unique blend of content (for example, home décor, cooking, fashion, relationships) for younger women. Sous Style rapidly gained influence online, receiving national recognition one year after launching. Lord was named one of *Bon Appétit*'s Tastemakers 2012 ("visionaries who are making our lives so delicious") and Sous Style was recognized by *Forbes* as one of the top ten Parenting and Homemaking Websites for Women in 2012. In 2014, Lord was one of the featured speakers at the Mom 2.0 Summit, a conference for the most influential women entrepreneurs who create online content.

Now that Lord is an entrepreneur responsible for hiring and managing her own team, she cites social skills as a prime asset she considers when evaluating potential employees. She looks for people who appreciate the importance of social conventions, such as knowing to say "thank you." While personalities differ, she deems it critical that people at Sous Style be pleasant and, in fact, "cheery" when working with others. Talented young people who land interviews with her would do well to remember people's names and faces and lend a personal touch to their interactions. And they should bear in mind that these behaviors will be required on a daily basis *after* they're hired.

As Lord has discovered, strong social skills can propel progress in a career. Further, they matter when you are out in front, running your own business and building your own team. Clients who enjoy working with Lord want to work with her more. Team members who welcome her leadership look forward to seeing her every day. While business professionals need all kinds of skills to be effective, influential leaders, Lord contends that "people will support you if you know how to behave well and, simply put, know how to get on with everyone." Jen wholeheartedly agrees, adding that getting along with others helps reinforce the idea that you really do care about their well-being. Such concern, in the end, is what employers seek in new hires, and what makes a great manager, executive, and yes, entrepreneur. Each of these roles requires a sensitivity not just to one's own needs, but to the interests and feelings of others as well.

## Likeability: A Slippery,
## but Important, Concept

Let's be clear: In talking about social skills, we're referencing a set of common behaviors that transcend any differences we might find in personality traits or levels of gregariousness. We can define social skills broadly speaking as things people do to make themselves "likeable." Likeability, however, can be a slippery concept, and in particular there has been much debate as to whether it's inherently gendered. In her bestselling book *Lean In*, Sheryl Sandberg, COO of Facebook, contends that women leaders are perceived as less "likeable" than men. She cites research suggesting that traits admired in men take on negative connotations when attributed to women. In the famous "Heidi and Harold" case study conducted at the Harvard Business School, one group was given a report on the successful career of the entrepreneur Heidi Roizen. A second group was given the same material but with one key difference: The entrepreneur's name was changed from "Heidi" to "Harold." Despite *the same exact* information on the entrepreneur, "Heidi" was perceived much more negatively than "Harold."

Some have questioned this research, arguing that likeability and success go hand in hand for both men and women. In the *Harvard Business Review* blog, Jack Zenger and Joseph Folkman have presented evidence that, they contend, contradicts Sandberg's position and reveals a strong link between success and likeability for both genders. Rather than seeking to resolve this debate, we simply observe that "likeability" can mean two different things: the degree to which people literally "like" someone, or a constellation of people skills that make people socially effective. In this chapter, we do touch on the first of these meanings, but we focus primarily on the second.

## Likeability in Childhood = Success in Adulthood

"Likeability" becomes such an important concept for parenting because influential research on children has depicted it as a strong predictor of life trajectory—including professional success and psychological adjustment. A study published in *Development and Psychopathology* followed a group of more than 200 schoolchildren for over twenty years. Researchers hypothesized that emerging "social competencies" in childhood (that is, people skills) have a long-term "cascade" effect on adult development, enabling kids to adapt positively at a number of key developmental stages. The data bore this out: While academic attainment in childhood represented one key factor influencing a positive trajectory, another was the overall level of social competence with peers. High levels of social competence led to successful work histories in adulthood; problems with peers signaled eventual work difficulties.

Another team of Canadian researchers followed a cohort of more than 300 individuals from childhood through age thirty-five. During childhood, the children's social competence with peers was assessed and broken down into three components: aggression, withdrawal, and likeability. While literature suggests that high levels of aggression and withdrawal during childhood can negatively impact adulthood, less attention has been paid to the effects of likeability. Researchers defined likeability as the extent to which other children liked to spend time with a child *and* a child's ability to form friendships. To get this information, peer ratings were collected in the classroom for each child. In past research, soliciting the opinions of peers has proven reliable and productive as a research method.

Researchers came to a striking conclusion: The more likeable a child was rated, the lower his or her risk of psychiatric disorder was in adulthood. A child's likeability corresponded to what researchers termed "positive resources in adulthood"—attributes and achievements that seemed to "buffer" adults from negative experiences and problems. One such resource was the number of years of education completed, while a second was a high rating on the Occupational Prestige Scale, a quantitative index of occupational status. Children who were rated as highly likeable were also likely to pursue high-status jobs as adults.

It's critical to recognize that in these studies, likeability is not the same as being "popular." Many kids in a given classroom are rated as being likeable by their peers, while only a few are considered to be the most "popular" personalities. To bring in an old-time phrase, likeable kids are those who are perceived to be a "good egg." You can be somewhat shy *and* likeable, and you can also be somewhat assertive. Likeability transcends specific personality traits—it's about an ability to get along well with those around you. And these three longitudinal studies suggest that school years are a critical time in which children either do or don't develop the people skills that often lead to adult work satisfaction, performance, and success.

## The 3 "C Words" That Make a Difference

Imagine you're starting a new business. You're going to need a variety of people with a range of vocational skill sets, and these individuals at some point are going to have to interact with one another. The team developing your product or service (whatever it is) has to know how to work collaboratively to solve problems; they also have to be able to have meaningful, focused exchanges with people in every department. If some employees aren't focused on the work at hand, if they distract others and pick fights, you will have lots of drama to worry about, making it that much harder to build a successful enterprise.

These same dynamics arise in classrooms, too. Kids exist in social networks; school amounts to a natural laboratory where they can develop the ability to function well in groups. Likeable kids, from the perspective of their peers, are those who know how to behave appropriately at different times of the day. During recess, they know how to play. When the teacher is giving a lesson, they know how to focus on the work. When it's time to work in small groups, they are respectful of others' ideas and know how to share their own. And when conflicts arise, likeable kids can work through them in a productive way. All throughout the day, likeable kids get a boost, simply because they're not chafing against their social environment.

It might seem obvious that likeability leaves kids happier. But it contributes to a child's overall academic success as well. Children's capacity to "do well" in the classroom depends heavily on interactions with other kids. Kids who aren't listening or following directions are often distracted, in part, by other kids. Kids who constantly interrupt when other students are speaking not only disrupt the class but also interfere with their own opportunities to learn through listening. Kids who want to dominate a group project—or who consistently withdraw from it—miss out on collaborative learning. And those who constantly disagree and argue with other kids don't develop the interpersonal skills that are required later in life.

Aware of just how much academic success hinges on social proficiency, educators are now working on large-scale efforts to bolster young children's social and emotional skills. The Collaborative for Academic, Social, and Emotional Learning (CASEL), led by Dr. Roger Weissberg at the University of Illinois at Chicago, helps states across the country integrate effective social and emotional learning programs within their academic curriculum. The work of CASEL—which is based on more than two decades of research—reinforces the idea that while people skills aren't the "soft" abilities we think they are (as opposed to "hard" cognitive/intellectual skills), they really matter. Data from organizations like CASEL show how interventions focusing on social and emotional learning lead to improvements in grades and performance on standardized tests. "Soft" people skills directly influence the development of "hard" cognitive abilities.

What can parents do to promote people skills in their children? Our answer is the three C's—Collaboration, Conflict, and Conversation. Each of these terms captures a dimension of social proficiency that can blossom in the home across the ages, positioning kids to succeed later in life. Let's take a look.

## Collaboration: Working with Others

One of the earliest things a child learns in the home is how to work with others. You might not think about it this way, but if you have a toddler, the simple act of shopping for groceries becomes a potential exercise in collaboration. Talking to your toddler about the grocery list and what products you're looking for engages them in the task at hand. She becomes easier to manage in the store as she internalizes grocery shopping as an activity you can accomplish together. When you involve her by asking her to help find items, to place manageable products in the basket, and to empty your cart onto the conveyor belt at the register, she is collaborating. You have just taken what might otherwise have been a battle of wills and self-interest and turned it into a team effort. You can easily apply this approach to any other activity suitable for young children, such as cooking, cleaning, or washing the car. Everyday exercises in collaboration can take place at any age. As kids' capacities increase, their ability to collaborate does as well.

To grasp how well you and your child are collaborating, you might try a simple experiment that researchers use. In studies that examine family functioning, parents and children are often given tasks to complete which provide insight into their ability to function as a unit. One typical task is to ask family members to jointly plan a meal; they are usually given five minutes to do so. The research team then observes the extent to which family members are simply *endorsing what they like* versus *creating a meal that pleases everyone.* Try this yourself at home: Do you find yourself dictating components of a meal, or are you and your children designing a meal that merges your (often quite different) tastes? If the former, then you might want to try slowing down, taking a deep breath, listening to your child more, and involving him in the creative process.

A focus on collaboration can also help parents handle the dynamics of sibling relationships. We are all aware of sibling rivalry, but one of the concrete challenges parents face is managing the competing demands of siblings. Issues that may seem relatively minor when occurring between friends—like where to go for a meal or what movie to see—can create constant stress between siblings. A parent can set the tone and framework for collaborative thinking by laying down a few rules. Rule Number One: *Nothing* fun is going to happen unless a collaborative solution is reached. Rule Number Two: Collaboration involves *talking,* not yelling. And Rule Number Three: Some kind of compromise should be established and the *kids* should be the ones to broker it. With these rules in mind, try planning a vacation together. Are you arriving at solutions that satisfy the competing demands of siblings?

Socializing a child to collaborate with other children can dramatically shape their future social behavior. Take sharing. In Richard's surveying of popular writings, he's seen the pendulum swing between the idea that young children are inherently selfish and hence shouldn't be *asked* to share and the concept that if you *don't* teach sharing at a young age, children will grow up to be selfish. In his view, both perspectives have merit. With young children, you want to cultivate sharing while simultaneously having patience and recognizing it as an emerging skill. Young children are learning to coordinate their own interests with the interests of others, and to understand that both interests matter. We don't want to raise kids who are predominantly "pleasers," constantly deferring to the wishes of others, any more than we want them to always try to get what they want at the expense of others. Sharing resides somewhere between the two.

During his years as a graduate student, Richard spent a lot of time observing preschoolers in action. His mentor, Dr. Melanie Killen, developed a task in which three preschoolers would sit at a table and be given a fixed number of toys to play with. Richard and Dr. Killen would then observe a mixture of sharing and competition. In the schools, we watched teachers letting kids work out their own solutions (which they did, some of the time), intervening only if the situation seemed to be getting out of hand. Teachers would gently prod and remind children to figure out a solution, as opposed to just offering one. This is a good strategy to keep in mind; young kids teach themselves when they try to work out their *own* ways to share. They won't succeed every time, but emphasizing sharing's importance prods them to figure out how to collaborate with others and leads to deeper learning (as opposed to just doing what they are told to do).

You might also try explicitly exposing your child to the benefits of taking turns. If your child is at the playground, you want him to understand that *he* wouldn't be happy if he didn't get a turn on a swing, so he should be motivated to let others have a turn as well. If he finds that someone else is not sharing with him, he should simply ask—in a friendly way—if he can have a turn. These techniques remain helpful as kids get older. In middle and high school, kids have to make all kinds of decisions about how to structure their time and maintain equitable relationships. Which movie should she see with her friends? Where should she go to eat? Remind your children of the rules we outlined to help moderate sibling relationships. Emphasize that *nothing* fun is going to happen unless a collaborative solution is reached, that collaboration involves *talk* and not yelling, and that kids need to broker their own compromises. Help create a climate of collaboration that will carry into the classroom and children's later social relationships. And note that collaboration is flagged as one of the "twenty-first-century skills" that are proposed to take on added importance in the future life of a child.

Help create a climate of collaboration.

We live and work in an increasingly collaborative world, and building such competencies throughout childhood will undoubtedly come in handy later.

## The Art of Managing Conflicts

Knowing how to handle and resolve conflicts when they arise is another core people skill—one that parents, with the right approach, can cultivate in the family. Dr. Diana Baumrind identified several distinct parenting styles derived from two important characteristics: warmth and control. *Warmth* captures the emotional tone of the parent-child relationship—the degree to which parents respond emotionally to their children and accept their behavior. *Control* refers to the essential parenting task of managing a child's behavior. Some parents are strict and rigid, others fairly loose with rules and demands. An overall *parenting style* reflects the ways in which parental warmth and control come together.

Baumrind captured the range of possible styles as a two-by-two table in which a parent is coded as being either high or low on warmth and control. As this typology of parenting style has been highly influential in academics, and is still frequently cited in writings and discussions about parenting, it's useful to know the key descriptors. *Authoritative parents* combine high warmth with firmness in managing their child's behavior. *Authoritarian parents* are low on warmth *and* strict in managing behavior; they don't show affection spontaneously with their child and do not respond to their child's emotional needs.

*Permissive parents* are warm and caring, perhaps to an extreme; they are sometimes overly indulgent, especially because they don't do much to establish and enforce rules. *Uninvolved parents* are very low on warmth, to the point of being disengaged and disinterested in their child's life.

An extraordinary number of studies performed over the past three decades have examined the effects of these types of parenting styles on children's development. The vast majority of papers suggest that *authoritative parents* confer the most developmental advantages to their children. Their children learn how to negotiate social interactions, have productive discussions, handle conflicts and disagreements, and form and maintain positive close relationships. One of the key ways authoritative parents accomplish this is by modeling and teaching self-regulation, particularly when conflict arises. Conflicts often happen—and escalate—because negative emotions dominate the expression of differing opinions. While authoritative parents hold firm on select rules and standards, they also encourage conversation about the *reasons* behind the rules, listening to their children's opinions. And after careful consideration, if there is a good reason to modify something based on their child's reasoning and information, they will do so. Conflicts get discussed, viewpoints get exchanged, and resolutions are offered based on an evaluation of *all* the information.

Not all parents embrace this approach, though. Authoritarian (as opposed to authoritative) parents often think that their hardline approach is necessary to make children behave properly and responsibly. In truth, children raised by authoritarian parents often have difficulty controlling themselves. Kids will model their parents' hard-line mentality and insist, in the classroom and on the playground, that there is only *one* way to do things; to them, conflict resolution means trying to get one's way, using whatever means necessary. Meanwhile, kids raised in a permissive household *expect* to get their way; therefore, they have more trouble connecting with peers, navigating social challenges, and forming good working relationships with teachers.

The effects of parenting style on a child's social skills can be seen early in their schooling. One study tracked the development of nearly 7,000 infants until their entry into kindergarten. Researchers collected extensive data on the parent-child relationship, particularly measures of emotional supportiveness and responsiveness as indicators of parenting style. The results were clear. Parenting practices consistent with authoritative parenting predicted children's social competence when they entered kindergarten. These kids were better able to overcome conflict and manage disagreement at school.

While Baumrind's typology has been around for many years, it remains centrally important because it helps us address difficult social issues affecting today's youth. It has been extremely useful, for instance, in helping us understand the dynamics of bullying, which after all is an extreme form of conflict between kids. According to the National Center for Education Statistics, the number of teenagers who reported bullying increased by nearly 25 percent between 2002 and 2007. As of 2013, almost one-third of the children sampled reported being bullied during the school year. This data likely understates the real problem, since many kids who are bullied don't ever report it.

The more socially adept kids are, the more they can avoid being bullied and cope with it if it does occur. Any amount of added protection can make a big difference, since research shows that the consequences of bullying can extend far out to adulthood. One group of researchers gathered a group of children ages nine to sixteen years of age and followed them into adulthood. As they reported in the journal *JAMA Psychiatry*, youth who reported being bullied during the school years were at increased risk for a number of psychiatric disorders in adulthood. Another paper from this study documented that these children also were *significantly less likely to hold down a job* in adulthood, as compared to children who were not bullied, and that bullied children also had substantial problems in maintaining social relationships.

A number of researchers have investigated the social dynamics that can help prevent bullying. Here parenting style again becomes critically important. A team of scholars analyzed a large number of studies conducted between 1970 and 2012, examining the links between parenting behavior, the risk of becoming a victim of bullying, and the ability to cope with the social challenges that arise in schools. Again, the results were clear: *Authoritative parenting strategies* (behaviors including good communication with children, warmth and affection, appropriate levels of support and involvement) protected children from the adverse effects of bullying. Parents pursuing these strategies nurtured a range of social competencies that made kids less likely to be victimized and more likely to cope with bullying when it happened. The practical implications are clear: Parents can help protect kids against bullying by embracing the elements of authoritative parenting: setting expectations and limits, providing contingencies when limits are tested, engaging in conversation, and showing plenty of affection, including emotional responsiveness to your child's needs and joys.

Not all research into conflict during childhood has centered on the styles of individual parents. Dr. Gerald Patterson, founder of the Oregon Social Learning Center (OSLC), focused his research on a family dynamic called "coercion." In families with coercive tendencies, requests tended to turn into demands, which turned into arguments and verbal tugs-of-war. The family members who persevered the longest in these arguments "won." Think about a father asking a five-year-old to turn off the television and put away his toys. The child yells "No!" and the father raises his voice. His initial request now becomes a harsh demand: "Turn that TV off *now* and put those toys away!" This leads to another "No!" from the child, and negative emotions escalate. The father might say: "If you don't turn that off, you won't be able to watch your show later tonight!" The child continues to say "No!" Inevitably, the parent gets exhausted—and the child continues to watch TV. The child comes away with some unhelpful lessons: that *conflicts are battles*, and wearing someone down is how you get your way.

In families where such behavior patterns have taken root, the solution is to learn strategies for avoiding the spiraling of hostility. Dr. Patterson's strategies are useful in a variety of scenarios. Here they are, tailored to the conflict over turning off the TV:

» Ask your child to turn off the TV because she needs to put away her toys—the toys are in the way, can get broken, and need to be put back in their proper place.

» If the child says "No!" calmly remind her that she can watch TV later, after the toys are put away. Ask her if there is a reason why they can't stop watching right now. If she offers a legitimate one, consider it—as long as you then expect her to follow through when the show is over.

» If you just get another "No!" simply say that if she doesn't turn off the TV and put away her toys, she will not be allowed to watch TV for the remainder of the night. And the key thing—the make-or-break moment—is to *follow through on that.* No exceptions. If that's the deal, that's the deal.

A few exchanges like this, and your child will eventually catch on. Provide a reason, remain calm, put in a contingency if necessary, and follow through. The "follow through" part of this cannot be overemphasized as it probably won't be pleasant the first few times you do this. However, over time your child will learn a form of conflict resolution applicable at any age and in any situation—a teen who chafes against a curfew, for instance, or a middle schooler who doesn't want to do her homework. It's a lesson in proactive negotiation, embracing exchanges of viewpoints, and transparently working toward equitable solutions.

## The Art of Conversation

Teacher Paul Barnwell, writing in *The Atlantic*, described his experiences explaining to teen students that they were going to "practice a skill they all desperately needed: holding a conversation." He contends that conversational competence may be the "single most overlooked skill we fail to teach students." It's easy for parents to cultivate conversational skills in their children simply by talking with them. Yet research continually shows that parents vary in how and how much they talk to their children in the early years of life.

In one in-depth study, eighteen-month-olds wore a specially designed shirt that recorded all the sounds they were exposed to during ten hours at home. Specialized software analyzed the sounds, picking out human speech and even distinguishing it from voices on televisions, radios, or computers. While one child heard 12,000 words of speech, another heard *less than 700 words*. The amount of child-directed speech directly predicted a toddler's vocabulary at twenty-four months and was associated with how quickly a child could process words in the laboratory. Only "real" talk produced benefits—background noise from television was, in fact, "noise" and not a "signal" that promoted speech skills.

Vocabulary growth and cognitive processing capacity are just some of the immediate language benefits of talking to babies and toddlers. By talking *to* and not *at* toddlers, we enable them to learn the social and linguistic elements of extended conversation. Parents of young children can practice performing "expansions"—literally, expanding on what the child says. If a child says "doggie," a parent can expand by saying "cute doggie." This conveys to the child not only that the parent is interested in what he or she is saying, but that conversation involves building on each other's talk. This technique works—in fact, it's a method that language interventionists often use to help children with communication difficulties. Research has shown that expansions lead children to extend their own contributions to the conversation and offer topical responses. Other conversational strategies include "wh-questions"—questions starting with "what," "where," or "why." Wh-questions inspire toddlers to expand as well.

Interestingly, some research suggests that expansions *without* wh-questions are the most effective stimulus for promoting conversational abilities in children. That said, even young children can be encouraged to respond to wh-questions (as well as other types of questions) and follow the rules of conversation when they are out with you. In the supermarket, you may be ordering cheese or turkey, and if you have a young child with you, he may be asked if he would like a slice. Encourage your child to answer for himself. Toddlers are perfectly capable of saying "yes, please" and "thank you." Socializing them to do this in public gets them in the habit of having simple conversational exchanges that are socially meaningful and appropriate. One note here: Telling your child "say thank you" doesn't count unless your child *actually* says it. It's easy for parents to get in the habit of talking *for* children, when, in fact, they can talk for themselves.

Keep an eye open to it, and you'll find many other opportunities for your child to engage in basic conversational exchanges. Children can be encouraged—and expected—to order for themselves in a restaurant. At a doctor's appointment, they can use their own words to explain why they are there—pediatricians often like to ask the child directly and encourage the child to answer. When you socialize with friends or relatives, your children can also become part of the conversation. If they are asked how school is going, teach them to give an expanded answer rather than just "good." Here they can also practice the art of *asking* questions and demonstrating interest in the lives of others. These are all simple ways, across many ages, that kids can learn and practice how to hold a meaningful conversation in the real world.

One factor can impede parent-child conversations: time. Kids and parents lead busy lives, making it tough to find time for deep, one-on-one conversation. A solution is to emphasize family dinners. Many studies have found that having dinner together leads to positive outcomes for children and teenagers, such as fewer emotional and behavioral problems. While family dinnertime can be spent in many ways—it can, for example, be oriented around watching television—the benefits seem to come when time is devoted to *conversation*. One study of more than 26,000 teenagers offered a fine-grained analysis, suggesting that the more dinners held per week, the stronger the beneficial effect. Each additional dinner was statistically associated with fewer emotional and behavioral problems and more trusting and helpful behaviors toward others.

However, if family dinners are to serve the function they are proposed to have, family members need to turn off the electronics and rely on old-fashioned talk. The mere fact of sitting together and consuming food is not enough; actual conversation and positive interaction are vital. Families can, of course, find other times to promote their conversations. They can block time on weekends that are "device free." Playing board games can also serve as a backdrop for spontaneous talk. The overarching goal is to find *and embrace* uninterrupted time for families to talk and share together on a regular basis.

## Communication Skills in Today's Virtual World

Conversational skills lay a cognitive foundation for children to communicate well with others. Communication in turn requires that children understand one another's thoughts and emotions and express their *own* thoughts and emotions. But communication is more than that—it reflects a social orientation that results in a useful connection between individuals. "Great communication skills are so empowering," reflects Pippa Lord, founder of Sous Style. "They are a way for people to learn about who you are, which helps them trust you and cultivate a deeper relationship. They help you gather followers, including the people who work with you and those you serve through your work. If you can communicate well, people will want to support you, and they will feel supported by you."

Today's youth will be asked to communicate in a number of ways, including electronically. Lord uses all forms of modern social media (for example, Facebook, Twitter, and Pinterest), bringing a definable and unique personality to her Sous Style lifestyle website. While some may regard social media as an artificial and impersonal way of communicating, it is a reality of modern life. Treating it as "just another microphone for people to use"—as described by Lord—is a positive way for parents to think about how kids can learn to express themselves and learn a whole other set of people skills. Social media and other forms of electronic communication provide young people with both an opportunity and a challenge. They *can* use these mediums to connect meaningfully with others, but doing so requires that they master new and rapidly evolving communication skills.

Other observers have elaborated on this point, paying special attention to what it takes to build a successful career. Online tips on how to interview on Skype can be found, and the website DailyMotion's segment "The Ticket to Career Success? Likability" focused on the increasing importance of videoconferencing and social networking, as well as the very real challenges of achieving "virtual likeability." Columnist Sue Shellenbarger and Tim Sanders, author of *The Likeability Factor*, detailed how hard it can be to seem authentic, take turns, and appear focused when we are participating in videoconferencing. They presented a number of tips (such as making eye contact, trying to smile naturally, varying tone of voice) that help to make virtual interaction more successful. It seems that achieving likeability in the workplace *now* hinges not merely on one's childhood experience (as revealed in the research), but on one's facility with video and social media platforms.

Skeptics wonder whether all this electronic interaction truncates children's communicative abilities and detracts from their overall social competence. Judith Shulevitz, writing in the *New Republic*, describes how a whole generation of children is growing up conducting "existential conversations with an iPhone," asking Siri questions and providing feedback on her answers. Querying a number of experts, Shulevitz found widespread concern that this form of interaction with artificially intelligent sources may eventually diminish the role of emotion in communication.

Does research offer us any guidance in this area? Dr. Sara Konrath, a social psychologist and professor at the University of Michigan, has offered a cogent review of relevant literature to date. She considers it possible that social networking sites may be promoting more self-orientation and less connection with others by encouraging superficial communication. She notes, however, that the existing research is far from conclusive, and that the lack of evidence can be taken as "leaving open more optimistic possibilities for new social media." While we wait for the research to catch up, parents would do well to help children cultivate a wide range of communication skills. Rather than write off social media, we should acknowledge that kids will have to learn *multiple* forms of effective communication. It's interesting to consider the experiences of younger professionals like Lord, since they have developed effective and meaningful ways of using the full spectrum of communication tools. As Lord reflects, "These evolving forms of communication will require social skills that have always been important, but will need to be honed in new ways."

As a parent, don't just "monitor" your child's media; become an astute reader of it. Identify the different sites your child may be using and get a sense for your child's online behavior. Is she pursuing *healthy* communication with peers? Are her texts and posts respectful? Is there evidence of gossip, rumor, or snarky commentary? Do they focus more on endorsing what she likes as opposed to attacking what she doesn't like? Most of all, does your child sound like *herself* on social media—what you might hear when she's hanging out with her friends or talking on the phone? Or is she saying things she'd never say to someone's face? Used in a healthy way, social media can help kids *find* their real voices in relation to other kids. It can help them grow as people, setting them up—as all healthy social interaction does—for a lifetime of success. "In these electronic and social mediums," Lord remarks, "it's easy to tell what's genuine, and what's not. As you learn to use tools like Twitter and Skype, you can be engaged in a process that helps you build the self. You can actually continually learn more about who you are and who you want to be." And, we might add, how to get along well with others and be "liked."

## Those First Job Interviews: A Test of People Skills

We've focused on social skills throughout childhood. Let's jump ahead to the endgame in many parents' mind: life after college. Public relations expert Faye de Muyshondt—author of *social-sklz:-) (Social Skills) for Success: How to Give Children the Skills They Need to Thrive in the Modern World* and founder of socialsklz:-) for SUCCESS—taught public relations and marketing classes at New York University, and it was here that she discovered firsthand just how much value social skills hold for graduating college seniors. In an interview with us, she explained that she encountered a number of students who had top grades but weren't getting job offers. Probing into this trend, Faye found that these talented, motivated, and successful students were missing one thing—they did not interview well. They might have had positive and meaningful relationships with friends, family members, and others in their lives, but they did not possess the people skills required to stand out in an interview against other equally attractive applicants.

After observing this phenomenon multiple times, de

Muyshondt created a class for college students called "The Brand Called YOU," teaching essential social and communication skills students would need to excel in interviews *and* in their chosen professions. She covered basic topics in conversational etiquette, such as eliminating phrases such as "like," "ya know," and "um" that don't play well in professional settings. Other fundamental social skills she taught included those that impact those "First Impressions"—including body language, facial expressions, and eye contact. She also covered electronic issues such as how to send an appropriate email and what to post and not post on social media.

De Muyshondt noticed a change in her students: They were getting better results in interviews! So she went on to create programs to develop social skills for a variety of age groups through her business, socialsklz:-). She explained to us that her work is founded on three principles:

» Social skills impact a child's developmental trajectory as well as their personal and academic successes.

» Social skills don't receive enough attention in school curriculums.

» Parents need to prioritize them as enthusiastically as they do academics and extracurricular activities.

In effect, de Muyshondt has built a successful business around the notion we've been positing in this chapter: that it's well worth a parent's time to cultivate people skills from toddlerhood to young adulthood. These skills set individuals apart in the workplace—not merely during interviews, but throughout a person's life on the job. As Jen tells her own staff, they need to be "binders"—people who build deep relationships with clients, colleagues, and others. Successful binders listen harder, care more deeply, and are more alert to what other professionals *really* need. They are great communicators and can handle differences of opinion and disagreements. They can build a relationship with *anyone*, inspire confidence, and are likeable; as a result, clients and colleagues want to be around them and feel bound to the firm. Binders have figured out that relationships enhance the quality of work, and, in general, they make the workplace a happier, more fulfilling place to be. Helping our own kids to develop into binders when they grow up will give them an essential skill set for navigating their world successfully.

# 7

‖‖‖‖‖‖‖‖‖‖‖‖‖‖‖

## SERVING OTHERS

We've seen that helping children cultivate a number of entrepreneurial tendencies or traits can position them well to eventually define and pursue their vision of success. But there is one tendency above others that entrepreneurial thinkers endorse as key to achievement: serving others. Look at any profession, and you'll find that if you don't somehow deliver value—if you don't contribute something that is wanted or needed—you can't succeed. Doctors heal people. Chefs make food people like. Artists move people emotionally. Success doesn't happen in isolation; people build businesses and careers by helping others and improving their lives. Dave Kerpen, founder and CEO of the marketing firm Likeable Local, suggested that the most important phrase you will ever say in a meeting is: "How can I help you?"

Businesspeople talk a lot these days about "purpose-driven

organizations"—organizations that seek to do more than just make money. But entrepreneurs have always been driven by higher purposes. Although they certainly want to make money, they intuitively understand that financial imperatives alone are not enough to carry businesses forward, and, in fact, their primary motivations in starting businesses often have little to do with profit. Jen's experience is a good example. Early in her career, Jen discovered that most people don't like their jobs very much. She decided that she wanted one day to create an organization where people looked forward to coming into work on Monday morning—a place where employees could thrive personally and professionally, where they did meaningful work, and where they felt that they were contributing powerfully to something important. Years later, when she founded her firm, she had a business plan that accounted for how the firm would turn a profit, but her vision of creating a better workplace remained the driving force. She has loved the challenge of running her firm, because she feels she has been able to see her vision come to life before her eyes. Her employees may not be pulling people out of burning buildings or curing cancer (as one of her colleagues says, "We're doing PR, not ER"), but they *do* perform meaningful work, and they are able to grow as people. They enjoy coming into work each week, and as a result, so does Jen.

## Being Valuable:
## Knowing What Others Want

How do entrepreneurs know which businesses to start? How do they find higher purposes to pursue? As Sheree Spoltore will tell you, crafting a vision like Jen's is not an easy thing to do; you have to work at it. Spoltore is the founder and president of Global Songwriters Connection (GSC), a premier songwriters' organization in Nashville, Tennessee. GSC offers a wide range of services to help songwriters improve their craft and increase their odds of competing successfully in the highly competitive music industry—their mission is to encourage, equip, and empower creators to be working and making a living with their gifts. Spoltore is well positioned for this entrepreneurial adventure, having achieved success herself as a songwriter, song plugger (the person who connects songs to artists), and mentor (she served seven years as the national director of membership and assistant executive director of membership for the Nashville Songwriters Association International (NSAI), the world's largest songwriter association). In that last role, Spoltore developed many programs for aspiring songwriters, resulting in hundreds of publishing deals for writers.

If you show up in Nashville with a guitar and a bunch of songs, you'll soon learn that you are not alone. There are an estimated 55,000 songwriters in the Nashville area. When Richard entered a 2009 meeting in Spoltore's NSAI office, he found it filled with piles of CDs. They were on Spoltore's desk, on shelves, in stacks on the floor—everywhere. She spoke eloquently of the challenges of trying to make your way in a town known for great songwriters: "The reality is that Nashville doesn't *need* another song. They have plenty of songs, plenty of great songs. Even if you build your skills so that you can write at that level, you will realize that writing great songs is not enough. You have to bring something else that Nashville doesn't have to make them *need you* via your songs."

In talking to us for this book, Spoltore expanded on this principle. "In business, you need to get in the habit of understanding the needs of others so you can meet those needs. Don't try to pitch someone a ballad if they are looking for an up-tempo song—and don't pitch an up-tempo that sounds like something they already have. This takes a particular kind of savvy that goes beyond the music. You need to put yourself in the other person's shoes and think about how you can help them. That's when someone in Nashville may find that they need you." Spoltore has it right: If you can figure out someone's needs, then all of a sudden your services become relevant. If we can help our kids get good at this, we'll be better able to launch them into a life that is satisfying, rich, and successful.

> You need to put yourself in the other person's shoes and think about how you can help them.

## Understanding and Embracing
## the Emotions of Others

While Spoltore works with people of all ages, she has spent considerable time with young people who are just starting to enter the music business. As a mentor, Spoltore doesn't just nurture musical talent—she also focuses on developing and honing young people's abilities to understand and embrace others' emotions. While emotional understanding is a large part of songwriting—Spoltore refers to songwriters as "architects of emotion"—it is also a tremendous asset in what is described as a "relationship town." In the music business, you have to collaborate constantly with other colleagues, and you can't do that well unless you can read their emotions. "Emotion understanding is a surprisingly important skill writers have to develop along with their song crafting skills," Spoltore says. "People want to be appreciated, recognized, and validated. They reveal themselves through their emotions. You need to know how to be appropriately read and react to their feelings—it's an important way of being valuable to them."

An extensive literature exists on the kind of emotional understanding that individuals must develop if they are to understand others' needs and emotions. It turns out that parents can do a lot to hasten this development in their children. Researchers have explored, for instance, the advantages and importance of talking to children about emotions, particularly in the early years of life. How parents communicate their own beliefs about emotions substantially impacts how kids grow up *thinking* about emotions. One interesting line of research has gauged whether parents consider emotions to be dangerous (something to be *avoided*) or adaptive (something to be *shared with others*). In filling out research questionnaires, parents who subscribe to the "danger" perspective might endorse sentences such as: "Children who feel emotions strongly are likely to face a lot of trouble." By contrast, parents who see emotions as adaptive would endorse sentences like: "It's important for children to express their happiness" or "Anger can be a useful motivation for action."

If parents signal that emotions are dangerous (for example, the idea that "if you follow your heart, and not your head, you will get hurt"), children will learn to dismiss others' emotions. They will tend to get "scared off" when someone is mad and, perhaps less obviously, if someone is gushing with happiness. Conversely, if parents signal that emotions are not just normal but important, kids not only develop healthy strategies for expressing their own feelings but also become attuned to observing and understanding the emotions of people around them.

Studies have demonstrated that parental beliefs about emotions predict their children's ability to understand others' emotions. For example, one project, published in 2014 in *Infant and Child Development*, studied parent-child dyads in the laboratory. Questionnaires allowed researchers to assess parents' beliefs about emotions as well as how much parents helped their children productively express emotions rather than hide them. Parents and children then participated in a number of emotion-related tasks, including watching videos that required children to identify the emotions being expressed. The results were clear: If parents valued emotions and guided children in navigating, their children were much more likely to correctly "read" the emotions of others in the videos. Children who learn that emotions are "dangerous" are at a disadvantage in learning how to perceive emotions in others.

## Probing Our *Own* Reactions

Think about your daily life as a parent. What do you do when your child gets angry or upset? Do you dismiss his feelings and act like he should get over it? Or do you acknowledge his feelings and discuss with him what is making him upset? Dismissing his anger affirms a sense of danger or negativity around emotions, while discussing it suggests to your child that attending to the feelings of others holds value, as does expressing his own feelings. Something similar holds true for positive emotions: Embracing the joy of your toddler affirms the importance of emotional sensitivity, while acting blasé disparages it. Now, busy parents obviously can't attend to every emotion expressed by a young child. But it's important

> Embracing the joy of your toddler affirms the importance of emotional sensitivity, while acting blasé disparages it.

to consider what you *typically* communicate to your child regarding emotions, especially those expressed by your child.

It's also critical to realize that you convey your beliefs about emotions when you talk about other people. Suppose Grandma clearly is not quite herself, and as a result, she isn't talking and playing as much with your child. You can help your child understand and embrace the emotions of others simply by connecting the dots for them (for example, "Grandma is quiet because she is sad—she found out a friend of hers is very sick"). Talking productively about your own emotions, of course, offers another powerful opportunity. It makes a difference if you say, "I'm upset because this company sent me the wrong item for the third time in a row—but I guess I'm going to call them back and maybe raise my voice a little to let them know how annoyed I am and that I want this handled right this time." You've let your child know that you aren't afraid of your feelings, that your feelings matter, that it's okay to express them, and that expressing them can usefully translate into action.

As children get older, and particularly in the early teen years, parental responses continue to shape how children sense and handle emotions. We all know that teens can react passionately to happenings that seem mundane to adults. Teens' emotions change quickly. Sometimes what they are feeling and how they express it seem detached from reality. While all this can feel taxing to a parent, it's important to sustain the positive message about emotions you broadcast. Try to lend a sympathetic ear if you can, and try your best not to act annoyed. Affirm to them that emotions matter—and that *their* emotions matter.

# Natural Helpers

Beyond emotional sensitivity, children are developing the ability to take action in response to emotions—in other words, to behave empathetically. One of the most important findings in developmental research is that toddlers (and perhaps even babies) possess a natural instinct to help, driven in part by their keen ability to recognize or infer that someone *needs* help. Researchers Felix Warneken and Michael Tomasello developed a clever experiment to test how willing *fourteen-month-olds* would be to provide help spontaneously. An experimenter simply dropped an object he or she had been holding in front of each of the toddlers. Many of the young toddlers picked it up and gave it back to the experimenter. Experimenters repeatedly demonstrated a need for help (for example, they lunged for a pen that was out of their reach) and toddlers provided that help (for example, they tried to get the pen for them). Critically, researchers made no explicit request for help. The toddlers simply observed that the experimenter needed help.

As other studies have shown, older toddlers are extremely savvy at not just wanting to help, but figuring out how to be most helpful. Yale University researchers Alia Martin and Kristina Olson created an experiment in which three-year-olds were asked for help, but the specific action they were asked to take wouldn't actually help the experimenter. For example, the experimenter asked the toddler to hand them a cup so they could pour water in it, but, in fact, the cup had a hole in it. In this situation, the toddlers did not comply, since they knew the broken cup would not aid the experimenter. However, in other situations, if the experimenter asked for a cup that was broken so they could throw it out, the toddler would give it to them. Martin and Olson describe this behavior as "paternalistic" helping, since the toddlers cared most about *truly* helping the experimenter rather than just complying with a request.

As this research suggests, the best way to enable children to develop as helpers is simply to give them the chance to offer assistance. This is important because busy parents may frequently feel that toddlers "get in the way" when something needs to be done. While parents sometimes do need to focus intensively on a task to complete it, they can still find plenty of opportunities to let young toddlers express their inclination to be helpers—and they can do this just by being present with their kids. They can perceive that you are "in need" and they want to help you as best they can. Asking for their help is certainly a good thing to do, but just *giving* them the chance to "serve" and affirming how much you like their service strongly reinforces their natural instinct.

In this regard, it's intriguing to loop back to the topic of chores, which we discussed in Chapter 5. There we landed on the idea that the best way to help kids reap the benefits associated with doing household chores was to nurture their internal motivation to do so. In collaboration with the Whirlpool Corporation, Richard has explored the idea that the most fundamental, and powerful, internal motivator may, in fact, be this idea that children are natural helpers. The proposition made in a white paper was that parents consider reframing perceptions of chores as opportunities for family members to help each other, and change their family conversations to reflect that mindset. Toddlers are certainly capable without prompting to pick up that shirt you dropped or grab that out-of-reach sock when you are folding the laundry. Children may certainly want to help you set the table or cook dinner. They may, in fact, be simply waiting for the opportunity to jump in and help.

Talking about chores as caretaking activities—ways in which every family member helps take care of each other, every day, as opposed to drudgery in the home—sets a family climate that encourages kids to follow their instincts to help. As described in the white paper, parents can talk about how they like making sure their kids have clean clothes that smell good, meals that they look forward to, and a house that looks inviting to their friends. And following through with simply including children at all ages in those everyday household activities as a positive family routine—rather than doling out responsibilities that are disconnected from a higher social purpose—can encourage their helping instincts to kick in. Just like the toddlers in the laboratory, kids don't want to be instructed to pitch in; they simply need to perceive the opportunity to do so, and then they will.

## Giving Older Children
## Opportunities to Do Good

Older children have a kind streak as well, but for them, life is more complicated. Competing demands such as homework or sports require focus, sometimes distracting them from helping others. Parents can help compensate by going out of their way to model altruistic behavior and to give their children opportunities to do good.

The Greater Good Science Center (GGSC) at the University of California, Berkeley, brings together scholars who study a wide range of prosocial behaviors. While acknowledging the inherent human tendency toward helpfulness, these scholars strongly encourage parents to cultivate kindness in children. Their website offers many useful tips for doing so. One of their suggestions is for parents to *model* kindness inside and outside the home. Parents might help others in public when they seem to be hurt or distressed or call 911 when they see a disabled car pulled over on the highway. Anything that acknowledges concern for others and models "helping" behavior sets a meaningful example for your kids. It's also important to spend time talking about what you are doing and why—to make explicit your understanding of someone else's plight and what action can make a difference.

The Greater Good Science Center also suggests involving children in volunteer activities. This can be done at home or with organizations, and in age-appropriate ways. You can participate in a bake sale, donate clothes to a local charity, or look for chances to provide canned foods to organizations that will distribute them to people in need.

If you are making a financial donation, make sure you articulate what you are doing and why. Actions speak louder than words, but it's still also important to talk about the empathic nature of

> Plant the seed of serving others *proactively.*

your behavior. The idea is to plant the seed of serving others *proactively.* And according to the GGSC, it is particularly important to involve the children in some type of *personalized* way. One of their more interesting suggestions is to have kids donate some of the Halloween candy they've collected to hospitalized children.

The GGSC recommends that parents not reward children for good deeds with money or gifts. Since the goal is for children to exercise their intrinsic desire to serve others, providing an external reward would be beside the point. But you should provide social reinforcement to children for their altruism. Although it is typically most effective to praise children's *effort* rather than the outcome of their action (or what those outcomes imply about their own personalities), we might make a subtle exception when trying to cultivate empathetic behaviors. Dr. Adam Grant (author of *Give and Take: Why Helping Others Drives Our Success*) described a few studies that support this conclusion in a piece for the *New York Times*. In one experiment, children won marbles in a game and donated some to poor children. Half of these children received praise for the *action*, while the other half received personal praise that indicated they were a nice and helpful person. Each child was brought back to the laboratory a few weeks later and provided more opportunities to give and share. The children who were personally praised for their prior giving were found to be *much* more generous. Grant notes that the type of language used can matter to young children—nouns like "helper" can be more influential than verbs like "to help." Again, this may be quite powerful to help children develop the self-concept of being an inherently giving person.

As a parent, try to find opportunities for your children to render service around and through their passions. Richard's daughter has always loved dogs, and he has fond memories of time his family spent volunteering in an animal shelter. The shelter had a volunteer program open to children of different ages, and shelter personnel screened the animals in advance to determine which ones would engage comfortably with young children. Parents and children underwent extensive training, after which they could come in at any time to take dogs for walks, bring them to fenced-in play areas, and train them to respond to simple commands. The shelter made it clear that the point was not just to give the dogs attention but to help social-ize them so that they could be placed in good homes. The whole family rejoiced in seeing a dog they had worked with leave with a new owner. Richard's daughter loved the shelter so much that she wanted to go every weekend and during school breaks. From the age of four, she found it one of her favorite activities.

# Three Acts of Kindness

Developmental studies suggest that prosocial behavior increases with age, and that tweens and teens naturally start to become sensitive to certain "rules" governing displays of altruism. For example, teens are more giving when they are with their friends. This makes sense; part of developing an intimate relationship involves wanting to do more for that person than acquaintances. What parents can do is help instill a sense of the *internal* reward that comes from helping others. Research conducted by Dr. Kristin Layous and colleagues provides a fascinating look at the positive effects that come from asking children to do good things for others. Nineteen classrooms in Vancouver, British Columbia, participated in the study. Children between nine and eleven years of age were divided into two groups. Each week for four weeks, one group was asked to visit three places (anywhere they wanted to go). The second group was asked to perform three acts of kindness. In-class surveys were used to gather information from the children on their assigned activities. Examples of places visited included "Grandma's house" and "a baseball diamond." Kind acts would be actions like "gave someone some of my lunch" and "gave my mom a hug when she was stressed." Prior to the four weeks of assigned activities, the children completed questionnaires that indicated their level of well-being. Students in each classroom also completed "sociometric" ratings of all of their classmates, indicating the students with whom they would like to spend time. At the end of the four weeks, all of these measures were taken again.

Being asked to perform acts of kindness led to an increase in well-being, but kids who were instructed to visit places also felt better about themselves. What distinguished the groups was that the children who performed acts of kindness saw increased peer nominations; their perceived *likeability* increased over the four weeks. As the authors suggest, creating classroom environments in which all kids are asked to perform acts of kindness may not only improve children's sense of well-being but make classrooms feel more inclusive. We agree and also suggest that a similar model might be brought into the home. A family that encourages "three acts of kindness" for *all* members may also substantially improve the general interpersonal dynamic at home.

## The Lemonade Stand: Much More Than an Early Business Opportunity

While most parents regard the nurturing of empathy, kindness, and prosocial behavior as a fundamental concern, the fact is that altruism in thought and deed also positions them for future success. Consider one of the archetypal symbols of the young entrepreneur, the lemonade stand. Opening a lemonade stand is one of the first experiences many kids have in trying to sell something. For some, like Brian Cunningham, it is transformative. Cunningham is the cofounder and CEO of My Career Launcher, an innovative venture devoted to cultivating entrepreneurial skills in children of all ages. As a kid growing up in Washington, DC, in the 1940s, Cunningham was easily distracted, found school boring, and could not see the point in learning something unless he was given a good reason. But something kicked in for him when he opened up a lemonade stand at the age of seven.

Cunningham remembers that even at that young age, he understood that he wasn't just selling lemonade—he was providing a service to others and, as such, had to consider their needs. In order to succeed in selling lemonade, he had to give customers more than lemonade; he had to provide some social reward as well. He recalls being interested in the people who came to his stand and enjoying the act of talking to them. Watching their eyes and their body language, he would notice that they *liked* buying lemonade from him. He came away from that experience with a principle he would use throughout his life: It's valuable to make people feel good.

> It's valuable to make people feel good.

More recently, having discovered that a significant number of successful entrepreneurs struggled at school or dropped out altogether, Brian became motivated to develop tools to help children of all ages learn entrepreneurial principles that could guide their development and career goals. My Career Launcher develops a comprehensive series of career guides to alert preschool, kindergarten, elementary, middle school, high school, and college students to the exciting career possibilities awaiting them.

My Career Launcher's first guide took the form of a book series for preschoolers. *Camila's Lemonade Stand* was inspired by Cunningham's reflections on the lessons he learned in Washington, DC, as a seven-year-old. Camila is one of "seven fearless children in search of their futures" who make up the Career Launcher Crew. The plot concerns a problem that Camila must solve by starting a business: A fair is in town with a thrilling Ferris wheel, but Camila doesn't have any money to ride it. She discovers, with the help of a "friendly sprite" named Itsy, that she can open a business—a lemonade stand. The book recounts problems encountered and solutions found, including the insight that figuring out how to provide something that others need is a path to success. In the end, Camila earns enough money to ride the Ferris wheel with her Career Launcher Crew friends.

Parents can use lemonade stands in other ways to instill a service ethic in their kids. A couple of years ago, the Kerpen family of Port Washington, New York, began taking weekly Saturday strolls down to the farmer's market in their town. Husband and wife Dave and Carrie (cofounders and CEOs of the social media agency Likeable Media) and their daughters, ten-year-old Charlotte and eight-year-old Kate, found that they enjoyed walking from stall to stall, talking to the farmers and bringing home fresh, organic produce to use in the family's meals. One Saturday not long after beginning this new family tradition, Charlotte became thirsty and wanted a drink. There were, however, no vendors selling beverages. A truck that sold smoothies had parked at the market a couple of times, but it was no longer there.

Charlotte brought the issue to the attention of her father. "That's quite a problem," he said. "How could we solve it?"

Charlotte thought for a moment. Her eyes brightened. "We could set up a lemonade stand!"

Dave thought this was a great idea and encouraged Charlotte to give it a try. As he explained to her, most lemonade stands are set up in front of someone's house. Their customers are mainly other kids and their parents. Setting up a lemonade stand at a farmer's market would address a real need there.

Charlotte had a lot of work to do to make this happen. Since the farmer's market was organic, she had to research how to create a truly organic drink. She had to come up with $25 to buy a license to sell at the market. And she had to figure out where best to position her stand. Every week during the summer, she got up early to make the lemonade and spent much of the day selling it. All her effort paid off. In fact, she made thousands of dollars in revenue during the summer. As Dave and Carrie recall, the episode was their "proudest entrepreneurial moment as parents." It wasn't about the money made. Rather, Dave and Carrie observed that Charlotte perceived a need that wasn't being addressed, developed a creative solution, and worked hard to make it a reality. Thanks to this experience, she internalized that first, most important question an entrepreneur asks: "How can I help you?"

The idea of kids using a lemonade stand to help others has also been featured prominently in a fascinating documentary called #standwithme, produced by Stillmotion, a unique filmmaking company based in Portland, Oregon. Grant Peelle, one of the filmmakers responsible for #standwithme, exemplifies the entrepreneurial habit of working to serve others. A husband and father to two young sons, he decided to give up his day job and pursue his passion of filmmaking. He wanted to focus on documentaries because he was particularly fascinated by people "who try to create a better world, and leverage their talents to do just that."

Peelle and his colleagues found one such story that was especially compelling. It concerned a young girl whose life was changed by seeing pictures of modern-day slavery in a museum. Here is the official synopsis of the documentary: "Only a nine-year-old would dream a lemonade stand could change the world. After seeing a photo of two enslaved boys in Nepal, Vivienne Harr is moved to help in the only way she knows how: by setting up her lemonade stand. With the goal of freeing 500 children from slavery, she sets up her stand every day, rain or shine." Without giving away too much of the plot, a key moment in the film has Vivienne coming up with a breakthrough idea for the lemonade stand: Rather than charging a fixed price, she offers buyers a chance to determine what they want to contribute to support the cause. In this way, she can appeal most strongly to their sense of altruism and let them reflect on why she is selling lemonade.

Not every child is going to start a business, let alone an altruistic one, but there are nonetheless moments in every child's life where she can and should internalize the link between succeeding in a venture and serving others. Maybe your child could sell candy for your church or synagogue, or hold a car wash to raise money to benefit communities in developing countries. Emphasize the good that money can do. Forge a link between something fun like candy or a car wash and a loftier end goal. Above all, help your kids to understand that others have needs just like they do, and that it is in satisfying those needs that we reap our own financial and emotional rewards.

## The Advantages of Being a Giver

We've referenced the work of Dr. Adam Grant, and here we highlight one additional finding from his influential research. Grant has proposed that "givers"—people who fundamentally enjoy helping others—often end up attaining substantial success over time. Discussing a subset of medical students who could be categorized as "givers," he notes that these students often spend hours providing help to their peers, even at the expense of their own grades. By the end of medical school, however, these givers are likely to have attained the highest grades. It may be that the passion these givers feel to help others also fuels their passion for learning medicine. Whatever the case, it certainly isn't true that "nice guys finish last." Altruism brings internal rewards of its own, but it also brings important and tangible external rewards as well. People succeed because they're able to better the lives of others.

Children will maximize their chances of achieving success by recognizing the unique value they offer others. This is especially true when it comes to getting into college. No matter the age of the child, most parents have college on their mind. And with good reason—we keep hearing about how the college application process continues to get more and more competitive. Many of the "elite" colleges have broken records for applications, and it's not uncommon for a school to receive well in excess of 30,000 applicants for a limited number of openings. For example, in 2014, Stanford University offered admission to 2,300 of the 32,022 students who applied (a 7.2 percent acceptance rate).

With admissions so tight, it's not surprising that students will try to tell colleges what they *think* they want to hear. It may surprise some parents and youth to learn that colleges place great value on potential contributions an applicant can make to the school community. Harvard University's website lists a number of factors admissions officers will take into consideration. Of course, grades, test scores, and letters of reference matter—a lot. But other factors matter, too. Admissions officers want to know what specific interests and talents a prospective student will bring and the extent to which those fit with the university. And they also want to know how a student will *function as a member of the Harvard community*, as reflected in the following questions asked in the application process: "Will you contribute something to Harvard and to your classmates? Will you benefit from your Harvard experience? Would other students want to room with you, share a meal, be in a seminar together, be teammates, or collaborate in a closely knit extracurricular group?"

Understanding that we are all here, in principle, to serve others is a powerful perspective. Success often happens when we figure out how we can bring value to other people's lives. Allowing this principle to guide our parenting won't guarantee that our kids will get into their dream college or get their songs recorded in Nashville. But it will position them to figure out how to eventually construct their *own* successful "lemonade stand"—the one that brings the most tangible value to their life and the wider community. It will position them to pursue a journey that leads to being happy, fulfilled, *enriched* adults.

# Epilogue

‖‖‖‖‖‖‖‖‖‖‖‖‖‖‖‖‖‖‖‖‖‖‖‖‖‖‖‖‖‖‖‖‖‖‖‖‖‖‖‖‖‖‖‖‖‖‖‖‖‖‖‖‖‖‖‖‖‖‖‖

## ENTREPRENEURIAL PRINCIPLES OF PARENTING

We wrote this book because we believed that the joint perspectives of an entrepreneur and a child development expert would yield useful strategies for parents struggling to raise kids in our fast-moving, uncertain era. We sought to help parents nurture traits that would enable kids to frame their own dreams and move proactively and energetically to realize them. Reflecting on the range of material covered in this book, we leave you with a few general principles to guide you in enhancing your current parenting behaviors.

# Principle 1:
# Our Seven Entrepreneurial Skills Overlap

Although the traits we've covered extend across cognitive, personal, and social domains, these traits also naturally connect with one another—in children's lives as well as in the lives of entrepreneurs. For instance, exploration leads to innovation. Optimism and opportunity seeking fuel both exploration and innovation. Industriousness—being a doer—helps us translate optimism into productive behaviors, and it also supports opportunity seeking. A majority of a child's cognitive efforts and personal attributes get expressed in social contexts, where they must collaborate and coordinate with others to fulfill their needs. Because entrepreneurial skills all intertwine, remember that as a parent you'll often be supporting (or thwarting) the development of multiple skills at once. Look for opportunities to achieve multiple victories, and also notice the intriguing and often surprising points of interconnection.

## Principle 2:
## Kids Pick Up Some Skills More Easily Than Others

Some kids seem like natural born optimists, while others tend more to pessimism. Some kids are inherently social; others may find social situations challenging. That said, every skill we talk about *is* teachable, and something parents can nurture to a significant extent. Shy kids may never become the affable, gregarious class president—but they can still absorb the social skills that will allow them to be more comfortable when interacting with others. Conversely, a child who seems to be naturally curious still needs to have that trait reinforced, cultivated, and not inhibited. As a parent, set reasonable expectations that conform to your child's natural inclination. Your goal is to enhance a skill, not necessarily turn it into your child's greatest asset. Improving abilities in an area that might not constitute a "strength" can make a huge difference in a child's life.

## Principle 3:
## Find Balance and a Middle Ground

Parents today are bombarded with polarizing messages about how involved they should be in their children's lives. Some experts claim that parents are the single most important influence in their children's lives; others will emphasize genetics or peer influence and brush off parents' impact as relatively minor. In truth, as we've seen repeatedly, a "sweet zone" of involvement exists. You want to render support and encouragement, and you want to be that safe home base from which your child can stretch cognitively, personally, and socially. You *don't* want to do your child's homework for her, or smother her with guidance, or do the myriad other things that overinvolved parents do.

As a parent, your ultimate goal should be to give your child sufficient opportunity to capitalize on his *own* abilities. Although that may sound like a major task, a moderate amount of support and encouragement goes a long way. Babies simply need to engage with you in order to develop their natural tendency to explore with their senses; you don't have to do anything more than play with them and take care of their needs, and you'll find that their exploratory behavior increases in sophistication throughout the first year of life. Likewise, we presented intriguing evidence that parents can foster innovation by supporting their child's play *without* directing it. The right kind of involvement makes all the difference.

# Principle 4:
## Focus on Process, Not Outcome

Culture today is obsessed with measuring kids' progress. Preschoolers are screened with standardized assessments. School-age kids—and schools—are subjected to all kinds of formal testing. And, of course, there is the grueling college admissions process. In this context of testing and more testing, it's understandable that parents feel pressure to "prepare" their children for success measured in terms of grades and scores. In truth, though, many essential skills fostered by parents aren't typically captured by these tests, though their importance is revealed when they are captured in research. The scientific literature as well as the life stories of entrepreneurs suggest that honoring your child's fundamental needs to develop cognitively, personally, and emotionally is the best way to promote the very success that all the "measurements" are supposed to predict. In education, there is talk—and perhaps a growing trend—to include more authentic assessments of all the skills that children need to develop, including those covered in this book. But for the time being, when you worry about the pressures of making sure your child "performs well" and has the right numbers as currently assessed, rest assured that the strategies we endorse promote life skills your children can use every day and, in fact, predict many of those eventual "outcomes" that we all want for our kids. Also know that you don't always need to measure your child's exploration and immediately validate it against some external standard. Focus on process, not outcome.

# Principle 5:
# Invest in Your "Can-Do" Child

In our Introduction, we acknowledged how difficult it now is for children to gain entrance into their desired schools and to find the right job after graduation (or any job, for that matter). The sheer intensity of competition might discourage parents or even lead to the occasional bout of panic. Without at all dismissing or diminishing parents' concerns, we've tried to suggest that the best way to proactively give your child an edge is to invest in him. Give children the cognitive, personal, and social skills to make their way through all these very real challenges so that they can define and pursue successes on *their* terms. It's a difficult, ever-changing world that awaits our children. Equipping them with the skills that help them become "can-do" kids is the very best investment you can make.

# ACKNOWLEDGMENTS

This book was the result of many conversations. Richard and Jen were introduced by Lorin Rees, who saw the potential in merging Jen's ideas about raising entrepreneurial children with Richard's perspectives on research and evidence-based practice. Lorin shepherded the evolution of the book's concept and brought much professional wisdom and passion to the quest of finding the synergy in our collaborative voice, and in keeping the train on the tracks and moving toward publication. He also brought a very real perspective as a parent to the continuous task of evaluating the utility of the material we considered.

Seth Schulman, who had an initial conversation with Jen and brought the idea to Lorin's attention, played a pivotal role by offering his expertise in every stage of the writing. He devoted countless hours (in person, on the phone, via email) brainstorming and riffing on the vision of the book, the structure and content, and the writing itself, with passion, creativity, high standards, encouragement, and good humor. He also brought stellar editorial expertise to the manuscript throughout, along with his colleague Christine Allen.

Susan Etkind offered another dedicated and inspired voice to the many conversations that supported the development of the book. She brought a needed perspective on entrepreneurship combined with outstanding editorial skills to find the connections between entrepreneurial concepts and parenting. Her consistent presence and effort were essential ingredients in keeping the process moving toward a collaborative point of view.

Marian Lizzi provided exemplary editorial skill to ensure the ideas got expressed in a meaningful way for parents and those who take great interest in how we raise children. She was quick to call out too much academic jargon and keep the focus on presenting technical material in the service of offering helpful ideas and supporting information to inspire parents and caretakers. Her deep reads and rapid assimilation of material drawn from many disciplines led to many probing questions and suggestions, and her expert editing sharpened the content throughout the writing process.

We had the good fortune of having many conversations with amazing people who are featured in this book. Every interviewee was generous not only with time but also with passion in sharing their life stories, insights, and professional perspectives. They brought enthusiasm while making time for introductory and preparatory email exchanges, in-depth phone conversations, and follow-up correspondences. By sharing the lives they have led, they provide a heart and soul to the book along with road-tested principles.

Richard thanks his wife, Cheryl, and daughter, Iliana, for supporting the late nights and weekends that provided the time for writing, and for the shared experiences that offered reflection on parenting and what it is like growing up these days. A special nod goes to Carlo, the ever loyal and joyful Westie, who was a constant companion for the writing sessions. He knew when to just hang, and also knew when it was time to take a walk and ponder the night sky.

# NOTES AND RESOURCES

## INTRODUCTION

**"twenty-first-century skills"** See, for example, the work of the Partnership for 21st Century Skills, p21.org.

**a world of "can and can-nots"** A white paper (*The Future Hunters*, Whiteboard Quarterly Trend Summit, December 15, 2014) summarized the perspectives offered at the Trend Summit meeting hosted by Weiner, Edrich, Brown Inc.

## 1. WIRED FOR EXPLORATION

**Dan Harple** Email exchanges and phone interview with author, May 2014.

**American Academy of Pediatrics (AAP) published a detailed report on data suggesting that free play** "The Importance of Play in Promoting Healthy Child Development and Maintaining Strong Parent-Child Bonds," Kenneth R. Ginsburg et al., *Pediatrics*, 2007, 119: 182–91.

**public radio station KUOW Puget Sound reported** "Recess Shrinks at Seattle Schools; Poor Schools Fare Worst," Ann Dornfeld, kuow.org/post/recess-shrinks-seattle-schools-poor-schools-fare-worst, May 14, 2014.

another report by the AAP (published in 2013) "The Crucial Role of Recess in School," Council on School Health, *Pediatrics*, 2013, 131: 183–88.

How about canceling the school play in kindergarten Consider, for example, the reaction from Diane Debrovner, deputy editor of *Parents* magazine: "It's Crazy to Worry About College in Kindergarten," Diane Debrovner, parents.com/blogs/parents-perspective/2014/04/28/the-parents-perspec tive/its-crazy-to-worry-about-college-in-kindergarten, April 28, 2014.

giving young children *freedom to choose from a range of hands-on activities* "The Impact of Pretend Play on Children's Development: A Review of the Evidence," Angeline S. Lillard et al., *Psychological Bulletin*, 2013, 139: 1–34.

Josh Levs has proposed parental anxiety as the primary factor behind such overstructuring "Overscheduled Kids, Anxious Parents," Josh Levs, cnn.com/2013/03/08/living/overscheduled-busy-children/index.html, March 10, 2013.

Catherine Clifford, writing on Entrepreneur.com "Why Everyone Will Have to Become an Entrepreneur (Infographic)," Catherine Clifford, entrepreneur.com/article/228176#ixzz2eJFMvuhl, September 3, 2013.

a paper published in *Evolutionary Psychology* "Children's Risky Play from an Evolutionary Perspective: The Anti-Phobic Effects of Thrilling Experiences," Ellen Beate Hansen Sandseter and Leif Edward Ottesen Kennair, *Evolutionary Psychology*, 2011, 9: 257–84.

Dr. Colin DeYoung, an expert researcher in this area "Openness/Intellect: A Dimension of Personality Reflecting Cognitive Exploration," Colin G. DeYoung, in M. L. Cooper and R. J. Larsen (assoc. eds.), *APA Handbook of Personality and Social Psychology: Personality Processes and Individual Differences* (Vol. 4), 2014, Washington, DC: American Psychological Association.

Drs. Hao Zao and Scott E. Seibert analyzed the findings of twenty-three research studies "The Big Five Personality Dimensions and Entrepreneurial Status: A Meta-Analytic Review," Hao Zao and Scott E. Seibert, *Journal of Applied Psychology*, 2006, 91: 25–71.

The overarching conclusion from many "genetically informative" studies For example, a recent study of about 10,000 twins and siblings estimated the heritability of openness to experience to be 54 percent . . . "The Five-Factor Model of Personality and Borderline Personality Disorder: A Genetic Analysis of Comorbidity," Marijn A. Distel et al., *Biological Psychiatry*, 2009, 66: 1131–38.

**Like Goldilocks, babies have a sweet zone of what's "just right"** "The Goldilocks Effect: Human Infants Allocate Attention to Visual Sequences That Are Neither Too Simple nor Too Complex," Celeste Kidd et al., *PLoS ONE*, 2012, 7: e36399, doi:10.1371/journal .pone.0036399.

**While researchers have debated the meaning of "tongue protrusion" in newborns** "Imitation of Tongue Protrusion in Human Neonates: Specificity of the Response in a Large Sample," Emese Nagy et al., *Developmental Psychology*, 2013, 49: 1628–38.

**One experiment studied how intensely babies read the face as part of learning language** "Infants Display Selective Attention to the Mouth of a Talking Face When Learning Speech," David J. Lewkowicz and Amy M. Hansen-Tift, *Proceedings of the National Academy of Science*, 2012, 109: 1431–36.

**CSM has been tracking, via nationally based surveys, changes in children's media use over the past few years** "Zero to Eight: Children's Media Use in America 2013," Common Sense Media Research Study, Fall 2013.

**As described by Vicky Rideout, research director for CSM** "New Data Reveal How Dominant Screen Time Is in Kids' Lives," Richard Rende, parents.com/blogs/red-hot-parenting/2013/10/30/health/new-data -reveal-how-dominant-screen-time-is-in-kids-lives, October 30, 2013.

**In 2013, the American Academy of Pediatrics (AAP) issued new guidelines** "Children, Adolescents, and the Media," Council on Communication and Media, *Pediatrics*, 2013, 132: 958–62.

**Drs. Michele Lobo and James Galloway provided a group of parents/ caregivers with three weeks of training** "Enhanced Handling and Positioning in Early Infancy Advances Development Through the First Year," Michele A. Lobo and James C. Galloway, *Child Development*, 2012, 83: 1290–1302.

babies who ranged from 4.5 to 7.5 months were brought into a laboratory where researchers observed how they visually and manually explored play objects "Systems in Development: Motor Skill Acquisition Facilitates Three-Dimensional Object Completion," Kasey C. Soska et al., *Developmental Psychology*, 2010, 46: 129–38.

Wells cites her experiences as a parent Email, phone, and in-person interview with author, December 2013.

The overall vision is to "foster a joy of learning." Children's Museum of Phoenix, childrensmuseumofphoenix.org.

Brigham Young University's student-produced news website "The Digital Universe" published a story "New Museum Expected to Combat Dwindling Creativity," Adam Mears, *The Digital Universe*, February 19, 2014.

In a study published in *Pediatrics*, nine focus groups comprised of child care teachers and providers "Societal Values and Policies May Curtail Preschool Children's Physical Activity in Child Care Centers," Kristen A. Copeland et al., *Pediatrics*, 2012, 129: 1–10.

Some experts are even worried that some toddlers may even be diagnosed incorrectly with ADHD "Expand Pre-K, Not A.D.H.D.," Stephen P. Hinshaw and Richard M. Scheffler, nytimes.com/2014/02/24/opinion/expand-pre-k-not-adhd.html, February 23, 2014.

the simple act of learning to copy basic shapes at ages two and three "Fine Motor Skills and Executive Function Both Contribute to Kindergarten Achievement," Claire E. Cameron et al., *Child Development*, 2012, 83: 1229–44.

A white paper offered by the research organization Challenge Success "Changing the Conversation About Homework from Quantity and Achievement to Quality and Engagement," Challenge Success, Challengesuccess.org/Portals/0/Docs/ChallengeSuccess-Homework-WhitePaper.pdf, 2012.

## 2. PRIMED TO INNOVATE

the American Public Media show *Marketplace* commissioned a survey "The Role of Higher Education in Career Development: Employer Perceptions," chronicle.com/items/biz/pdf/Employers%20Survey.pdf, December 2012.

Dr. Tony Wagner, expert in residence at Harvard University's Innovation Lab Email and phone interview with author, February 10, 2014.

In an interview with Thomas L. Friedman of the *New York Times*, Laszlo Bock "How to Get a Job at Google," Thomas L. Friedman, nytimes.com/2014/02/23/opinion/Sunday/friedman-how-to-get-a-job-at-google.html, February 22, 2014.

Po Bronson and Ashley Merryman, authors of the influential book *NurtureShock: New Thinking About Children* "The Creativity Crisis," Po Bronson and Ashley Merryman, newsweek.com/creativity-crisis-74665, July 10, 2010.

In his hugely influential TED talk titled "How Schools Kill Creativity," Sir Kenneth Robinson "How Schools Kill Creativity," Ken Robinson, ted.com/talks/ken_robinson_says_schools_kill_creativity, February 2006.

Dana Conover is Elmer's director of innovation and new products Email and phone interview with author, April 2014.

Joe Wetli, Elmer's director of innovation and new business development Email and phone interview with author, April 2014.

#Inspire 100 list singles out "thinkers, designers, and risk takers" who are "moved by their individual passions and who inspire others to do the same" "Kicking Off Inspired Gifting This Holiday Season, Dell Announces the #Inspire 100," dell.com/learn/us/en/uscorp1/secure/2012-11-20-dell-holidays-inspire-100, November 20, 2012.

Brooks focused on business in college, attending University of Michigan's Stephen M. Ross School of Business. She told us Email and phone interview with author, January 2014.

Harvard's Tony Wagner refers to as the triad of "play, passion, purpose" See Wagner's book, *Creating Innovators: The Making of Young People Who Will Change the World*, 2012, New York: Scribner.

as developmental psychologist Angeline Lillard has proposed, pretend is hardly the only way that kids can engage in creative thinking "The Impact of Pretend Play on Children's Development: A Review of the Evidence," Angeline S. Lillard et al., *Psychological Bulletin*, 2013, 139: 1–34.

Drs. Caren Walker and Alison Gopnik suggest that pretend "Pretense and Possibility: A Theoretical Proposal About the Effects of Pretend Play on Development: Comment on Lillard et al.," Caren M. Walker and Alison Gopnik, *Psychological Bulletin*, 2013, 139: 40–44.

An experiment performed by researcher Laura Schulz and colleagues at MIT "Where Science Starts: Spontaneous Experiments in Pre-schoolers' Exploratory Play," Claire Cook et al., *Cognition*, 2011, 120: 341–49.

Dr. Alison Gopnik and colleagues carried out a similar experiment with four-year-olds that yielded nearly identical results "Children's Imitation of Causal Action Sequences Is Influenced by Statistical and Pedagogical Evidence," Daphna Buchsbaum et al., *Cognition*, 2011, 120: 331–40.

A study published in *Parenting: Science and Practice* "Patterns of Maternal Directiveness by Ethnicity Among Early Head Start Research Participants," Jean Ispa et al., *Parenting: Science and Practice*, 2013, 13: 58–75.

an influential article in the *Harvard Educational Review* "Expanding Our 'Frames' of Mind for Education and the Arts," Jennifer S. Groff, *Harvard Educational Review*, 2013, 83: 15–39.

"Einstein was certainly not a standout in his mathematics and physics classes" "The Art and Craft of Science," Robert Root-Bernstein and Michele Root-Bernstein, *Creativity Now!*, 2013, 70: 16–21.

Dr. Juan Ivaldi, a highly successful and influential chemist and innovator, agrees Email and phone interview with author, April 2014.

Research conducted by Root-Bernstein with colleagues at Michigan State University "Arts and Crafts: Critical to Economic Innovation," Rex LaMore et al., *Economic Development Quarterly*, 2013, 27: 221–29.

Richard teamed with Elmer's Products See, for example, letsbond.elmers.com.

an informative blog post "Fueling Creativity in the Classroom with Divergent Thinking," Stacey Goodman, edutopia.org/blog/fueling-creativity-through-divergent-thinking-classroom-stacey-goodman, March 18, 2014.

In the book *The Innovator's DNA: Mastering the Five Skills of Disruptive Innovators* Jeff Dyer et al., 2011, Cambridge: Harvard Business Review Press.

Sheila Marikar, writing in the *New York Times* "The Lives of Millennial Career Jugglers," Sheila Marikar, nytimes.com/2014/12/07/fashion/the-lives-of-millennial-career-jugglers.html, December 5, 2014.

author Rick Newman has provided evidence "This One Uberskill Will Always Keep You Employed," Rick Newman, *Yahoo! Finance*, December 10, 2014.

## 3. RAISING OPTIMISTS

Swedish citizens were asked to gauge the state of their economy "The Bright but Right View? New Evidence on Entrepreneurial Optimism," Ola Bengtsson and Daniel Ekeblom, *Working Papers*, No. 2014:1, Department of Economics, Lund University, January 8, 2014.

William Frick, writing in the *Harvard Business Review* blog "Entrepreneurs Don't Have an Optimism Bias—You Have a Pessimism Bias," Walter Frick, hbr.org/2014/02/entrepreneurs-dont-have-an-optimism-bias-you-have-a-pessimism-bias/, February 13, 2014.

Psychologists Charles S. Carver and Michael F. Scheier "Dispositional Optimism," Charles S. Carver and Michael F. Scheier, *Trends in Cognitive Sciences*, 2014, 18: 293–99.

John Jacobs, cofounder (with his brother Bert) and chief creative optimist Email and phone interview with author, October 2012.

Lylah M. Alphonse, senior editor of "Yahoo! Shine" "Parents Who Hate Parenting: The Latest Trend?" Lylah M. Alphonse, https://ca.shine.yahoo.com/parents-who-hate-parenting--the-latest-trend-.html, March 21, 2011.

Jennifer Senior's bestselling book *All Joy and No Fun: The Paradox of Modern Parenthood*, Jennifer Senior, 2014, New York: Ecco.

Richard has conducted a number of studies of how depression "runs" in families For a brief summary of related studies, see *Psychosocial Interventions for Genetically Influenced Problems in Childhood and Adolescence*, Richard Rende, 2014, Hoboken, NJ: John Wiley & Sons.

Australian researchers examined nearly 4,000 pairs of adult twins "Sex Differences in the Genetic Architecture of Optimism and Health and Their Interrelation: A Study of Aging Twins," Miriam A. Mosing et al., *Twin Research Human Genetics*, 2010, 13: 322–29.

Researchers Michael Lorber and Byron Egeland examined data tracking 267 babies "Parenting and Infant Difficulty: Testing a Mutual Exacerbation Hypothesis to Predict Early Onset Conduct Problems," Michael F. Lorber and Byron Egeland, *Child Development*, 2011, 82: 2006–20.

researchers have turned to "hard puzzle" tasks See, for example, "Dyadic Flexibility in Early Parent-Child Interactions: Relations with Maternal Depressive Symptoms and Child Negativity and Behaviour Problems," Erika S. Lunkenheimer et al., *Infant and Child Development*, 2013, 22: 250–69.

As psychologists Carver and Scheier have written "Optimism," Charles S. Carver et al., *Clinical Psychology Review*, 2010, 30: 879–89.

A team of scientists tracked the progress of nearly 400 ten-year-olds "Life Stress, Maternal Optimism, and Adolescent Competence in Single Mother, African American Families," Zoe E. Taylor et al., *Journal of Family Psychology*, 2010, 24: 468–77.

another study used the same research approach "Dispositional Optimism: A Psychological Resource for Mexican-Origin Mothers Experiencing Economic Stress," Zoe E. Taylor et al., *Journal of Family Psychology*, 2012, 26: 133–39.

Qin believes this style of parenting is not optimal "Evaluating 'Tiger Mom' Parenting: What's the Take-Home Message from Research?" Richard Rende, parents.com/blogs/red-hot-parenting/2012/02/22/health/evalu ating-tiger-mom-parenting-whats-the-take-home-message-from -research/, February 22, 2012.

**Qin examined two groups of high-achieving kids** "Parent-Child Relations and Psychological Adjustment Among High-Achieving Chinese and European American Adolescents," Desiree Baolian Qin et al., *Journal of Adolescence*, 2012, 35: 863–73.

**Researchers at the University of Notre Dame found that kids (in second through ninth grade)** "Emergence of Attributional Style and Its Relation to Depressive Symptoms," David A. Cole et al., *Journal of Abnormal Psychology*, 2008, 117: 16–31.

**Researchers at the University of California, Davis, have broken new ground** "Looking on the Bright Side: Children's Knowledge About the Benefits of Positive Versus Negative Thinking," Christi Bamford and Kristin H. Lagattuta, *Child Development*, 2012, 83: 667–82.

**Dr. Robert Emmons, a leader in gratitude research** For an overview of Emmons's work, visit his website, gratitudepower.net/science.htm.

## 4. OPPORTUNITY SEEKERS

**Hanna Rosin, writing in *The Atlantic*** "The Overprotected Kid," Hanna Rosen, theatlantic.com/features/archive/2014/03/hey-parents-leave -those-kids-alone/358631, April 2014.

**A study published in *Pediatrics*** "Societal Values and Policies May Curtail Preschool Children's Physical Activity in Child Care Centers," Kristen A. Copeland et al., *Pediatrics*, 2012, 129: 265–75.

**The National Childcare Accreditation Counsel of Australia** "I'm Not Scared: Risk and Challenge in Children's Programs," Anne Kennedy, *Putting Children First*, 2009, 31: 9–11.

**Malcolm Gladwell has argued** "The Sure Thing," Malcolm Gladwell, newyorker.com/magazine/2010/01/18/the-sure-thing, January 18, 2010.

**Researchers Anna Macko and Tadeusz Tyszka** "Entrepreneurship and Risk Taking," Anna Macko and Tadeusz Tyszka, *Applied Psychology*, 2009, 58: 469–87.

as the influential pediatrician Dr. Harvey Karp suggests Email and phone interview with author, May 2014.

Accidental drownings are the second leading cause of death "Unintentional Drowning: Get the Facts," Centers for Disease Control and Prevention, cdc.gov/HomeandRecreationalSafety/Water-Safety/waterinjuries -factsheet.html.

A study published in the *American Journal of Sports Medicine* "National High School Athlete Concussion Rates from 2005–2006 to 2011– 2012," Joseph A. Rosenthal et al., *The American Journal of Sports Medicine*, April 16, 2014, doi:10.1177/0363546514530091.

Alan Tortolani became frustrated by the lack of productive educational games Email and phone interview with author, April 2014.

Attachment theory, as it is called, dates back to the seminal work of John Bowlby in the 1970s For example, *Attachment and Loss*, Vol. 2, *Separation*, John Bowlby, 1973, New York: Basic Books.

A research method called the Strange Situation For example, *Patterns of Attachment: A Psychological Study of the Strange Situation*, Mary D. S. Ainsworth et al., 1978, Hillsdale, NJ: Erlbaum.

Decades of research have shown that the Strange Situation offers prediction For example, "Conceptualizing the Role of Early Experience: Lessons from the Minnesota Longitudinal Study," L. Alan Sroufe et al., *Developmental Review*, 2010, 30: 36–51.

A recent study published in the *Journal of School Psychology* "The Relation of Parenting, Child Temperament, and Attachment Security in Early Childhood to Social Competence at School Entry," Kristin M. Rispoli et al., *Journal of School Psychology*, 2013, 51: 643–58.

Jerome Kagan coined the phrase "behavioral inhibition" decades ago For example, "Behavioral Inhibition to the Unfamiliar," Jerome Kagan et al., *Child Development*, 1984, 55: 2212–25. For recent research in this area, see onlinelibrary.wiley.com/doi/10.1002/icd.v23.3/issuetoc.

the Early Growth and Adoption Study "Intergenerational Transmission of Risk for Social Inhibition: The Interplay Between Parental Responsiveness and Genetic Influences," Misaki N. Natsuaki et al., *Development and Psychopathology*, 2013, 25: 261–74.

Dr. Diane Benoit uses the example of crying in the first year of life "Infant-Parent Attachment: Definition, Types, Antecedents, Measurement and Outcome," *Paediatric Child Health*, 2004, 9: 541–45.

Claudia Hepburn is the executive director and cofounder of the Next 36 Email and phone interview with author, February 2014.

Carolyn O'Laughlin, director of residence life at Sarah Lawrence College "'Snowplow' Parents May Be Trapping Their Children," Carolyn O'Laughlin, washingtonpost.com/opinions/snowplow-parents-may-be-trapping-their-children/2013/12/20/4eceb40c-6749-11e3-8b5b-a77187b716a3_story.html, December 20, 2013.

Startling data offered by sociologists Keith Robinson and Angel L. Harris "Parental Involvement Is Overrated," Keith Robinson and Angel L. Harris, opinionator.blogs.nytimes.com/2014/04/12/parental-involvement-is-overrated, April 12, 2014.

John Jacobs, cofounder and chief creative optimist of Life is good, likewise embraces mistakes Email and phone interview with author, October 2012.

Dr. Carol Dweck has performed decades of cutting-edge research See, for example, *Mindset: The New Psychology of Success*, Carol Dweck, 2007, New York: Ballantine Books.

## 5. DOERS

We approached Khosrowshahi for an interview Email and phone interview with author, December 2013 and January 2014.

"The Evidence for Generation Me and Against Generation We" "The Evidence for Generation Me and Against Generation We," Jean Twenge, *Emerging Adulthood*, 2013, 1: 11–16.

Dr. Jeffrey Jensen Arnett was not convinced "The Dangers of Generational Myth-Making: Rejoinder to Twenge," Jeffrey Jensen Arnett et al., *Emerging Adulthood*, 2013, 1: 17–20.

A few longitudinal studies illustrate the importance of performing chores "The Misperception of Chores: What's Really at Stake?" Richard

Rende, 2014, white paper prepared for the Whirlpool Corporation; "The Developmental Significance of Chores: Then and Now," Richard Rende, *Brown University Child and Adolescent Behavior Letter*, 2015, 31: 1, 6–7.

**a multidisciplinary examination of middle-class families in Los Angeles** "Children and Chores: A Mixed-Methods Study of Children's Household Work in Los Angeles Families," Wendy Klein et al., *Anthropology of Work Review*, 2009, 30: 98–109.

**An intriguing paper by Dr. Michael Inzlicht and colleagues** "Why Self-Control Seems (But May Not Be) Limited," Michael Inzlicht et al., *Trends in Cognitive Sciences*, 2014, 18: 127–33.

**Chores can become part of the social fabric of family time** "A Review of 50 Years of Research on Naturally Occurring Family Routines and Rituals: Cause for Celebration?" Barbara H. Fiese et al., *Journal of Family Psychology*, 2002, 16: 381–90; see also Rende, "The Misperception of Chores," 2014.

**Nick Sarillo, founder and CEO of two Chicago-area restaurants and author** Email and phone interview with author, December 2013.

**Josh Baron and Rob Lachenauer, writing in the *Harvard Business Review* blog** "Keep Your Kids Out of the Entitlement Trap," Josh Baron and Rob Lachenauer, hbr.org/2014/02/keep-your-kids-out-of-the-entitlement-trap, February 18, 2014.

**A working paper by Drs. Christopher Ruhm and Charles Baum** "The Changing Benefits of Early Work Experiences," Christopher L. Ruhm and Charles J. Baum, *NBER Working Paper 20413*, August 2014.

**as they begin to cultivate industriousness** "Conscientiousness: Origins in Childhood?" Nancy Eisenberg et al., *Developmental Psychology*, 2014, 50: 1331–49.

**the critical importance of "intrinsic motivation" throughout the formal school years** "Development of Achievement Motivation and Engagement," Allan Wigfield et al., in R. Lerner (Series Ed.) and M. E. Lamb and C. Garcia Coll (Volume Eds.), *Handbook of Child Psychology*, 7th Ed., Vol. 3, *Social, Emotional, and Personality Development*, in press, New York: John Wiley.

**Drs. Rebecca Shiner and Ann Masten have shown that the emerging motivation to master tasks** "Childhood Personality as a Harbinger of Competence and Resilience in Adulthood," Rebecca L. Shiner and Ann S. Masten, *Development and Psychopathology*, 2012, 24: 507–28.

**the research of Harvard's Dr. Roland Fryer** "Financial Incentives and Student Achievement: Evidence from Randomized Trials," Roland Fryer, *Quarterly Journal of Economics*, 2011, 126: 1755–98.

**Suzanne Cohon, who owns the prominent ASC Public Relations firm in Toronto** Email and phone interview with author, February 2014.

## 6. PEOPLE SKILLS

**When Pippa Lord was a college student in Australia** Email and phone interview with author, May 2015.

**In her bestselling book *Lean In*** See "For Women Leaders, Likeability and Success Hardly Go Hand-in Hand," Marianne Cooper, https://hbr.org/2013/04/for-women-leaders-likability-a/, April 30, 2013.

**In the *Harvard Business Review* blog** "New Research Shows Success Doesn't Make Women Less Likeable," Jack Zenger and Joseph Folkman, https://hbr.org/2013/04/leaning-in-without-hesitation, April 4, 2013.

**A study published in *Development and Psychopathology* followed a group of more than 200 schoolchildren** "The Significance of Childhood Competence and Problems for Adult Success in Work: A Developmental Cascade Analysis," Ann S. Masten et al., *Development and Psychopathology*, 2010, 22 (Special Issue 3): 679–94.

**Another team of Canadian researchers followed a cohort of more than 300 individuals** "Likeability, Aggression, and Social Withdrawal in Childhood, Psychiatric Status in Maturity: A Prospective Study," Alex E. Schwartzman et al., *European Journal of Developmental Science*, 2009, 3: 51–63.

The Collaborative for Academic, Social, and Emotional Learning (CASEL), led by Dr. Roger Weissberg See casel.org for an overview of accomplishments in both research and practice.

And note that collaboration is flagged as one of the "twenty-first-century skills" Partnership for 21st Century Skills, p21.org.

Dr. Diana Baumrind identified several distinct parenting styles derived from two important characteristics: warmth and control See, for example, "Effects of Authoritative Parental Control on Child Behavior," Diana Baumrind, *Child Development*, 1966, 37: 887–907; "The Influence of Parenting Style on Adolescent Competence and Substance Use," Diana Baumrind, *Journal of Early Adolescence*, 1991, 11: 56–95.

One study tracked the development of nearly 7,000 infants "The Relation of Parenting, Child Temperament, and Attachment Security in Early Childhood to Social Competence at School Entry," Kristin M. Rispoli et al., *Journal of School Psychology*, 2013, 51: 643–58.

According to the National Center for Education Statistics bullyingstatistics.org/content/school-bullying.html. For more recent statistics, see nces.ed.gov/fastfacts.

As they reported in the journal *JAMA Psychiatry* "Adult Psychiatric Outcomes of Bullying and Being Bullied by Peers in Childhood and Adolescence," William E. Copeland et al., *JAMA Psychiatry*, 2013, 70: 419–26; "Impact of Bullying in Childhood on Adult Health, Wealth, Crime and Social Outcomes," Dieter Wolke et al., *Psychological Science*, 2013, 24: 1958–70.

A team of scholars analyzed a large number of studies conducted between 1970 and 2012 "Parenting Behavior and the Risk of Becoming a Victim and a Bully/Victim: A Meta-Analysis Study," Suzet Tanya Lereya et al., *Child Abuse and Neglect*, 2013, 37: 1091–108.

Dr. Gerald Patterson, founder of the Oregon Social Learning Center (OSLC), focused his research on a family dynamic called "coercion" See, for example, an application to understanding sibling interaction, "Sisters, Brothers, and Delinquency: Evaluating Social Influence During Early and Middle Adolescence," Cheryl Slomkowski et al., *Child Development*, 2001, 72: 271–83.

Teacher Paul Barnwell, writing in *The Atlantic* "My Students Don't Know How to Have a Conversation," Paul Barnwell, theatlantic.com/educa tion/archive/2014/04/my-students-dont-know-how-to-have-a-con versation/360993/, April 22, 2014.

In one in-depth study, eighteen-month-olds wore a specially designed shirt "SES Differences in Language Processing Skill and Vocabulary Are Evident at 18 Months," Anne Fernald et al., *Developmental Science*, 2013, 16: 234–48.

Research has shown that expansions lead children to extend their own contributions "The Effects of Expansions, Questions and Cloze Pro cedures on Children's Conversational Skills," Tze-Peng Wong et al., *Clinical and Linguistic Phonetics*, 2012, 26: 273–87.

One study of more than 26,000 teenagers offered a fine-grained analysis "Family Dinners, Communication, and Mental Health in Canadian Adolescents," Frank J. Elgar et al., *Journal of Adolescent Health*, 2013, 52: 433–38.

the website DailyMotion's segment dailymotion.com/video/x1jouy2 _the-ticket-to-career-success-likability_news, March 25, 2014.

Judith Shulevitz, writing in the *New Republic* "Siri, You're Messing Up a Generation of Children," Judith Shulevitz, newrepublic.com/article/ 117242/siris-psychological-effects-children, April 2, 2014.

Dr. Sara Konrath, a social psychologist "The Empathy Paradox: Increasing Disconnection in the Age of Increasing Connection," Sara Konrath, in R. Luppicini (ed.), *Handbook of Research on Technoself: Identity in a Technological Society*, 2012, Hershey, PA: IGI Global.

Public relations expert Faye de Muyshondt Email and phone interview, May 2014.

## 7. SERVING OTHERS

Dave Kerpen, founder and CEO of the marketing firm Likeable Local "CEO: The Most Important Thing You Can Say at a Meeting," Dave

Kerpen, ragan.com/Main/Articles/CEO_The_most_important _thing_you_can_say_at_a_meet_46423.aspx, March 25, 2013.

As Sheree Spoltore will tell you Email and phone interview, December 2013 and January 2014.

One interesting line of research has gauged whether parents consider emotions to be dangerous "Parents' Beliefs About Emotions and Children's Recognition of Parents' Emotions," Julie C. Dunsmore et al., *Journal of Nonverbal Behavior*, 2009, 33: 121–40.

For example, one project, published in 2014 in *Infant and Child Development* "Parents' Emotion-Related Beliefs, Behaviours, and Skills Predict Children's Recognition of Emotion," Vanessa L. Castro et al., *Infant and Child Development*, Epub, May 14, 2014.

Researchers Felix Warneken and Michael Tomasello "Helping and Cooperation at 14 Months of Age," Felix Warneken and Michael Tomasello, *Infancy*, 2007, 11: 271–94.

Yale University researchers Alia Martin and Kristina Olson "When Kids Know Better: Paternalistic Helping in 3-Year-Old Children," Alia Martin and Kristina R. Olson, *Developmental Psychology*, 2013, 49: 2071–81.

In collaboration with the Whirlpool Corporation "The Misperception of Chores: What's Really at Stake?" Richard Rende, 2014, white paper prepared for the Whirlpool Corporation.

Greater Good Science Center (GGSC) at the University of California, Berkeley greatergood.berkeley.edu.

Dr. Adam Grant (author of *Give and Take: Why Helping Others Drives Our Success*) described a few studies "Raising a Moral Child," Adam Grant, nytimes.com/2014/04/12/opinion/sunday/raising-a-moral-child .html, April 11, 2014; for more on Grant's work, see nytimes.com/2013/ 03/31/magazine/is-giving-the-secret-to-getting-ahead.html.

Research conducted by Dr. Kristin Layous and colleagues "Kindness Counts: Prompting Prosocial Behavior in Preadolescents Boosts Peer Acceptance and Well-Being," Kristin Layous et al., *PLoS ONE*, 2012, 7: e51380, doi:10.1371/journal.pone.0051380.

**Cunningham is the cofounder and CEO of My Career Launcher** Email and phone interview, December 2013.

**Husband and wife Dave and Carrie (cofounders and CEOs of the social media agency Likeable Media)** Email and phone interview, January 2014.

**Grant Peelle, one of the filmmakers responsible for #*standwithme*** Email and phone interview, May 2014.

**Grant has proposed that "givers"** "How to Succeed Professionally by Helping Others," Adam Grant, theatlantic.com/health/archive/2014/03/how-to-succeed-professionally-by-helping-others/284429/, March 17, 2014.

# INDEX

academic performance
   homework and, 36
   parental behavior, impact on, 123,
      153–55
   small successes leading to, 126
   and social proficiency, 168–69
academic readiness
   free play role in, 3–5, 32–35
   predicting, 82
accountability, sense of, 148
adaptability trait, 6–8
adversity, dealing with, 84–86, 90–92
Ainsworth, Mary, 113–14
*All Joy and No Fun* (Senior), 77
allowances, 140
Alphonse, Lylah M., 76–77
altruistic behavior. *See* serving others
American Academy of Pediatrics (AAP),
      3–4, 17
*American Journal of Sports
   Medicine*, 107
Arnett, Jeffrey Jensen, 136
arts and crafts
   cognitive importance of, 60–64
   innovation linked to, 65–67
Asian American families, 87–88
"associating," concept of, 70–71
*Atlantic, The*, 179
attachment theory, 112–15

attributional styles, 90–91
authoritarian parenting, 173, 174–75
authoritative parenting, 173, 174, 175,
      176–77

babies
   exploration, cultivating in, 10–13,
      19–22
   "face-to-face interaction" with, 13–15,
      18–19
   screen time concerns, 14–18
Barnwell, Paul, 179
Baumrind, Diana, 173
behavioral inhibition, 115
Benoit, Diane, 116
binders term, 188
Bock, Laszlo, 40
boredom, parental responses to, 99–100
boundaries in exploration, defining,
      27–28
Bowlby, John, 112
Bronson, Po, 41
Brooks, Rachel, 45–49, 68–69
bullying, 175–77

"can-do kids," skills contributing to,
      xvi–xvii
   *See also specific skills*
Carver, Charles S., 74, 84

Center on Everyday Lives of Families
(CELF), 138–39
Centre for Curriculum Redesign, 60
Challenge Success, 36
Children's Museum of Phoenix (CMP),
23–24
children's museums
exploration in, 22–25, 26–27
home activities inspired by, 26–30
chores for children
children as natural helpers, 198–99
as internally rewarding, 140, 142–45
mandatory approach to, 141–42
promoting responsibility with, 138–40
Christensen, Clayton M., 70
Chua, Amy, 87
Citizen Made, 45–46
Clifford, Catherine, 6
"coercion" family dynamic, 177–78
cognitive skill
arts and crafts benefitting, 60–64,
65–67
in babies, 10–12, 12–13, 13–15
hands-on activities developing, 5
language development and, 13–14
motor development related to, 19–22
"openness to experience" as, 8–10
pretend play as, 52–54
screen time affecting, 14–15
in toddlers, developing, 23
See also innovation
Cohon, Suzanne, 158–59
collaboration, 169–73
Collaborative for Academic, Social,
and Emotional Learning (CASEL),
168–69
college admissions factors, 210–11
Common Sense Media (CSM), 15–16
conceptualization, 71
confidence, developing, 119–20
conflict management, 173–79
Conover, Dana, 44
contextual thinking, 44
conversational exchanges, 179–82
counterfactual reasoning
concept of, 53–54

deconstruction as, 58–59
divergent thinking related to, 66–67
encouraging in children, 54–57
modeling for children, 59–60
Creating Innovators (Wagner), 40
creativity
divergent thinking and, 66–67
educational crisis with, 41–43
in home setting, 48
pretend play influence on, 52
See also arts and crafts
critical thinking skills, 44
See also innovation
criticism, limiting, 128–29
Cunningham, Brian, 204–5

"daily innovation," practice of, 45
deconstruction, concept of, 58–59
depression risk, optimism effect on, 91
Development and Psychopathology, 165
DeYoung, Colin, 8
Dickson, Tom, 25
discovery
modeling, 55–56
supporting in children, 27
See also exploration in children
divergent thinking, 66–67
See also counterfactual reasoning
doers, children as, 131–59
chores, mandatory, 141–42
chores, parental strategies for, 142–45
chores promoting responsibility,
138–40
early work experiences, 148–51
entitlement, sense of, 132–35, 135–37
grades, 156, 157–58, 217
independence and self-sufficiency,
152–53
internal vs. external rewards, 140,
142–45
internships and volunteer
opportunities, 150–51
intrinsic motivation, 154–55, 157–58
narcissism and self-esteem, 135–36
observing/helping parents, benefits of,
145–47

parental interest in schoolwork,
156–58
"real world" transitioning, 158–59
schoolwork motivation and effort,
153–55
trait introduced, xv
Dweck, Carol, 126–27
Dyer, Jeff, 70

early childhood
arts participation, value of, 64
cognitive exploration, 23
*See also* preschool years; toddler years
educational systems
creativity and innovation in, 41–43
kindergarten classrooms, 4–5, 114–15
preschool years, 34, 53, 152–53
*See also* academic performance; grades
Egeland, Byron, 79–80
Einstein, Albert, 61–62
Elmer's Products Inc., 43–45, 65
*Emerging Adulthood*, 135, 136
Emmons, Robert, 98–99
emotions
acknowledging and communicating,
195–96
emotional understanding, developing,
193–95
empathetic behavior, 197–98, 201–2
responsiveness to child's, 116–18
*See also* optimism; pessimism
empathetic behavior, 197–98, 201–2
employment. *See* job opportunities;
workplaces
entitlement, sense of, 132–35
entrepreneurial principles, 213–18
finding balance and middle ground,
215–16
focusing on process, not outcome,
216–17
investing in your child, 218
setting reasonable expectations, 215
supporting multiple skills, 214
entrepreneurial skills
overview of, xiii–xv
supporting "can-do kids," xvi–xvii

entrepreneurial success
adaptability trait for, 6–8
coauthor's childhood innovation,
50–51
cognitive exploration and, 23
conceptualization and, 71
lemonade stand examples of, 204–9
"openness to experience" trait and,
8–9
opportunity seekers and, 103–4,
108–9, 110–11
optimism contributing to, 81
predictability concept and, 11–12
serving others and, 189–90
skills for success, summarized, 213–18
*See also* innovation
environment, exploring. *See* exploration
in babies; exploration in children
environmental influences, 77–78, 78–81
"Evidence for Generation Me and
Against Generation We, The,"
135–36
*Evolutionary Psychology*, 7
"Expanding Our 'Frames' of Mind for
Education and the Arts" (Groff),
60–61
exploration in babies
cultivating exploration, 12–13
"face-to-face interaction," 13–15,
18–19
"Goldilocks Effect," 10–11
information processing, 10–12
positioning babies, 19–22
predictability concept, 11–12
rooting reflex, 11, 13
screen time impacting, 14–18
selective perception, 11, 12
trait introduced, xiv
exploration in children
academic success through, 32–35
children's museums, 22–25
cognitive exploration, 23
free play role, 3–8, 28–29, 32–35
home activities for, 26–30
homework demands, 36–38
innovator's childhood recalled, 47–48

exploration in children (*cont.*)
limit setting, 27–28
"openness to experience," 8–10, 30–32
parental advocacy in schools, 37–38
redirection technique, 27–28
respect and tolerance, cultivating,
30–32
trait introduced, xiv
unstructured experiences, 1–3
*See also* hands-on learning

"face-to-face interaction," 13–19
failure
growth mindset and, 127–28
as learning experience, 124–26
family climate
family dinners, benefits of, 181–82
positivity impacting, 75–76, 76–78,
94–97
Folkman, Joseph, 164–65
free play
childhood benefits of, 3–8, 28–29,
32–35
leading to passion and purpose, 48–49
pretend play as, 52–53
*See also* exploration in children
Frick, William, 74
Friedman, Thomas L., 40
"frustration tolerance," 83
Fryer, Roland, 158
"Fueling Creativity in the Classroom
with Divergent Thinking," 67

Galloway, James, 20
genetic influences
behavioral inhibition and, 115
on optimism and pessimism, 77–78
personality traits and, 9–10
George Lucas Educational Foundation
(GLEF), 67
*Give and Take* (Grant), 201
Gladwell, Malcolm, 103
Global Songwriters Connection
(GSC), 191
"Goldilocks Effect," 10–11
Gopnik, Alison, 53, 55–56

grades
homework linked to, 36
perspective on, 156, 157–58, 217
*See also* academic performance
Grant, Adam, 201–2, 209
gratitude, cultivating, 97–99
Greater Good Science Center (GGSC),
200–201
Gregerson, Hal, 70
Groff, Jennifer, 60–61, 62
growth mindset, acquiring a, 126–28

"hands off, eyes on" parenting principle,
120–24
hands-on learning
deconstructing as, 58–59
need for, 25, 32–33
related to cognitive ability, 5
*See also* arts and crafts; children's
museums
Harple, Dan, 1–3
Harris, Angel L., 123
*Harvard Business Review*, 164
*Harvard Educational Review*, 60–61
Heidi and Harold case study, 164
"helicopter" parenting, 120, 153–54
Hepburn, Claudia, 117–18
high school years. *See* teenage years
homework
demands of, 36–38
parental involvement with, 123–24,
154–55, 156–57
"How Schools Kill Creativity"
(Robinson), 41

independence. *See* self-sufficiency and
independence, promoting
industriousness. *See* doers, children as
*Infant and Child Development*, 194–95
infants. *See* babies
information processing by babies, 10–13,
13–15
innovation, 39–71
the arts, impact on, 60–64, 65–67
"associating," concept of, 70–71
and career success, 39–41

conceptualization concept, 71
connection and integration leading to, 68–71
contextual thinking, 44–45
counterfactual reasoning, 53–54, 54–59
creativity crisis, 41–43
critical thinking skills, 44
"daily innovation" practice, 45
deconstruction leading to, 58–59
divergent thinking, 66–67
in educational systems, 41–43
fostering in children, 52–57
"pattern" concept, 68–69
restricting, 42–43
"thinking outside the box," 66–67
trait introduced, xiv
unstructured activities leading to, 48–49, 49–51
visualization process, 62–63
"whole mindedness" concept, 61
in the workplace, 43–45
young innovator's story, 45–47, 47–49
*Innovator's DNA, The* (Christensen, Dyer, and Gregerson), 70
internships and volunteer opportunities, 150–51
interview skills, 163, 186–88
intrinsic (internal) motivation
chores and, 140, 142–45
helping others, 198–99, 201–2, 203–4, 203–5
schoolwork and, 154–55, 157–58
in the workforce, 148–49
Inzlicht, Michael, 142
Ivaldi, Juan, 62–63

Jacobs, John, 75–76, 89, 96–97, 97–98, 100, 125
*JAMA Psychiatry*, 176
job opportunities
chores as, 140
in the classroom, 153
"dirty jobs," taking on, 134–35, 146–47, 148
early work experiences, value of

innovation ability for, 40–41
interview skills, 163, 186–88
parents, observing at work, 145–47
for teens, 148–51
*See also* workplaces
*Journal of School Psychology*, 114–15

Kagan, Jerome, 115
Karp, Harvey, 107, 119–20
Kerpen, Dave, 189, 206–7
Khosrowshahi, Golnar, 131–32, 137, 145–46
Killen, Melanie, 171
kindergarten classrooms
attachment theory related to, 114–15
curriculum, 4–5
kindness
acts of, 203–4
cultivating in children, 200
*See also* serving others
Konrath, Sara, 184–85

language development, 13–14, 179–81
Layous, Kristin, 203–4
learning. *See* academic performance; cognitive skill; hands-on learning
learning ability trait, 40–41
lemonade stands, 204–9
"less is more" principle
guiding and encouraging, 54–57
homework and, 36–37
linked to arts and crafts, 66
in the workplace, 57
Levs, Josh, 5–6
Life is good (lifestyle brand), 75
likeability concept
academic success and, 167–69
acts of kindness and, 203–4
adult success, predicting, 165–67
gender debate, 164–65
trait introduced, xv
"virtual likeability," 183–84
*Likeability Factor, The* (Sanders), 184
Likeable Local marketing firm, 189
Lillard, Angeline, 5, 52
limit setting in exploration, 27–28

Lobo, Michele, 20
Lorber, Michael, 79–80
Lord, Pippa, 161–63, 183, 185

Macko, Anna, 103–4
Marikar, Sheila, 71
Martin, Alai, 197–98
Masten, Ann, 154
mastery motivation, 154, 156
media use
    guidelines for, 17–18
    research on, 15–16
    screen time in infancy, 14–15
Merryman, Ashley, 41
middle school students
    conflict strategies for, 177–79
    homework and, 36–37
    negative attribution style in, 90
    See also teenage years
motivation. See intrinsic (internal)
    motivation; mastery motivation
motor skills, development of
    and academic readiness, 33–35
    cognitive growth and, 19–22
    crafting related to, 66
Museum of Natural Curiosity, 25
museums. See children's museums
Muyshondt, Faye de, 186–88
My Career Launcher, 205–6

narcissism in youth, 135–36
National Center for Education Statistics,
    175–76
National Childcare Accreditation
    Counsel of Australia, 102
negative attributional style, 90
    See also adversity, dealing with
negative behavior
    directiveness leading to, 56–57
    negative parenting promoting, 78–81
negativity
    family climate impacting, 77–78,
        90–91
    responding to in babies, 116–17
    risk-taking and, 102–3, 108–9
    See also pessimism

newborn babies. See babies
Newman, Rick, 71
New Republic, 184
NurtureShock (Bronson and
    Merryman), 41

O'Laughlin, Carolyn, 121–22
Olson, Kristina, 197–98
"openness to experience" trait, 8–10,
    30–32
opportunity seekers, 101–30
    attachment theory, 112–15
    behavioral inhibition, 115
    coauthor's experience, 150–51
    confidence, developing in children,
        119–20
    criticism, limiting, 128–29
    emotional responsiveness, 116–18
    entrepreneurs as, 103–4, 108–9,
        110–11
    failure as learning experience for,
        124–26
    future challenges for, 129–30
    growth mindset, 126–29
    "hands off, eyes on" principle, 120–24
    "helicopter" parenting, 120, 153–54
    minimizing risk, 105–6
    parental encouragement creating,
        126–29
    parental involvement with
        schoolwork, 120–24, 156–58
    risk, estimating, 106–8
    risk, rethinking, 108–9
    risk-taking avoidance, 101–3
    "snowplow" parenting, 121–22,
        153–54
    Strange Situation research method,
        113–14
optimism, 73–100
    adversity, enduring with, 84–86
    applying to events and situations,
        92–94
    Asian American families, 87–88
    boredom in kids, 99–100
    early parenting effect on, 78–81
    entrepreneurs as optimists, 73–74

environmental vs. genetic factors, 77–78
family climate, 75–76, 76–78, 94–97
"frustration tolerance," 83
gratitude, cultivating, 97–99
Life is good (brand) success story, 75–76
making good things happen trait, 99–100
negative attributional style, 90
optimistic vs. pessimistic approaches, 89–92
parental effect on, 78–81, 81–84, 87–89, 91–92
positive attributional style, 91
positive thinking, impact of, 94–97
research supporting, 73–74
tiger mom parenting, 87–88
trait introduced, xiv
Oregon Social Learning Center (OSLC), 177
overstructuring children, 5–6
See also structured activity

parenting
    entrepreneurial principles of, 213–18
    styles of, 87–88, 120–22, 173–75, 176–77
Parenting: Science and Practice, 56
"pattern" concept, 68–69
Patterson, Gerald, 177–78
Pediatrics, 102
Pediatrics, American Academy of, 3–4, 17
Peelle, Grant, 208
people skills, 161–88
    academic success tied to, 167–69
    authoritarian parents, 173, 174–75
    authoritative parents, 173, 174, 175, 176–77
    bullying behavior, 176–77
    in classroom environment, 167–68
    "coercion" family dynamic, 177–78
    collaboration, 169–73
    college admissions, 210–11
    college and beyond, 186–88

communication skills, 182–86
conflict management, 173–79
entrepreneur example of, 161–63
job interview/workplace skills, 186–88
language and conversation, 179–82
likeability factor, 164–65, 165–67, 167–69
parenting styles, 173–75, 176–77
permissive parents, 174, 175
sharing, cultivating, 171–72
sibling relationships, 170–71
social competence with peers, 165–67
social media, 183–86
uninvolved parents, 174
"virtual likeability," 183–84
permissive parenting, 174, 175
personal skills. See doers, children as; optimism; risk-taking
pessimism
    "fixed" mindset and, 127–28
    genetics role in, 77–78
    vs. optimism, 73–74, 89–92, 92–94
    See also negativity
play. See free play
positivity
    effect on babies, 79–80
    family climate and, 75–76, 76–78, 94–97
    modeling, 91–92
praise, role of
    and empathetic behavior, 201–2
    "fixed" mindsets, determining, 127
    related to chores, 143, 145
predictability concept, 11–12
preschool years
    arts participation, 64
    cognitive exploration, 23
    free play in, 33–34, 53
    independence and self-sufficiency, promoting, 152–53
    motor skills, developing, 35
    pretend play in, 53–54
    risk-taking observations, 102
    sharing, observations on, 171–72
    See also exploration in children
pretend play, 52–54

problem solving
  creativity reinforcing, 66
  guiding vs. teaching, 54–56
  *See also* counterfactual reasoning
Prosek, Jen
  childhood exploration, 22–23
  childhood innovations, 50–51
  creating opportunity, 69–70, 130
  "daily innovation" practice, 45
  failure as learning experience, 124–25
  gratitude and, 98
  independence and self-sufficiency, 152–53
  industriousness in workplace, 140
  "less is more" principle, 57
  "openness to experience," 8–9
  positive thinking, 95, 100
  "real world" experiences, 151
  risk-taking, 105–6
  workplace adaptability, 6
  workplace environment, 190
  workplace social skills, 188
prosocial behavior. *See* serving others
*Psychological Bulletin*, 5
purpose-driven organizations, 189–90

Qin, Desiree, 87–88

reading to toddlers, 35
recess time in schools, 4, 34
redirection technique, 27–28
Rende, Richard
  arts and crafts study, 65–66
  chores as opportunities, 198–99
  family climate, 77–78, 94–95, 96
  sense of entitlement, 133–34
  serving others, 202
  sharing, observations on, 171–72
  workplace opportunity, seizing, 150–51
  workplace sharing with kids, 147
research studies
  academics and social proficiency, 168–69
  acts of kindness, 203–4
  arts and crafts benefits, 65–66

arts involvement, 63–64
babies' facial bias, 13–14
behavioral inhibition, 115
on bullying, 176–77
children as natural helpers, 197–98
chores, 138–40
"coercion" family dynamic, 177–78
conversational competence, 179–81
counterfactual reasoning, 54–57
emotional understanding, 194–95
family interaction, 77, 182
genetic vs. environmental influences, 77–78
givers attaining success, 209
"Goldilocks Effect," 10–11
grades, rewarding, 157–58
on gratitude, 98–99
growth mind-set, 126–28
homework and academic achievement, 36–37
likeability, 164–65, 165–67
media use in children, 15–16
motor development and cognition, 20–21
narcissism and self-esteem, 135–36
"openness to experience," 8, 9–10
on optimism, 73–74, 77–78, 78–81, 81–83, 84–86, 89–92, 92–94
parental language and behavior, 90, 126–28, 179–81
parenting styles, 87–88, 175–77
playtime for children, 33–34
positivity and negativity, parental, 90
recess time, 4
risk-taking, 103–4
on sharing, 171–72
social competence with peers, 165–67
social media, 184–85
social proficiency and academics, 168–69
Strange Situation, 113–14
summer jobs, 149–50
Reservoir Media Management, 131–32, 145
respect and tolerance, cultivating, 30–32

rewards
    altruistic behavior and, 201–2
    for chores, 140, 142–45
    for grades, 157–58
    *See also* intrinsic (internal) motivation
Rideout, Vicky, 16
risk-taking
    entrepreneurs as risk-takers, 103–4,
        110–11
    minimizing risk, 105–6
    parents underestimating risk,
        106–8
    redefining, 108–9
    risk avoidance, 101–3
    trait introduced, xiv
Robinson, Keith, 123
Robinson, Kenneth, 41–42
Roizen, Heidi, 164
Root-Bernstein, Michele, 61
Root-Bernstein, Robert, 61, 63–64
rooting reflex, 11, 13
Rosin, Hanna, 101–2

Sandberg, Sheryl, 164
Sanders, Tim, 184
Sarillo, Nick, 146–47, 148–49, 150
Scheier, Michael F., 74, 84
schoolwork
    homework demands, 36–38
    parental involvement with, 120–24,
        156–58
    promoting motivation and effort for,
        153–55
    *See also* grades
Schulz, Laura, 54–55
sciences, role of the arts in the, 60–64
screen time, 14–18
Seibert, Scott E., 8
selective perception in babies, 11, 12
self-esteem in youth, inflated, 136
self-sufficiency and independence,
        promoting
    on the job, 148–49
    in preschoolers, 152–53
    "real world" examples, 158–59
Senior, Jennifer, 77

serving others, 189–211
    acts of kindness, 203–4
    children as natural helpers, 197–99
    chores as caretaking activities,
        198, 199
    emotional sensitivity, 195–96
    emotional understanding, developing,
        193–95
    entrepreneurs endorsing, 189–90
    giving, advantages of, 209–11
    internal rewards tied to, 203–4
    lemonade stand opportunities, 204–9
    meeting needs of others, 191–92
    older children, service for, 200–202
    trait introduced, xv
Shellenbarger, Sue, 184
Shiner, Rebecca, 154
Shulevitz, Judith, 184
sibling relationships, 170–71
*Slice of the Pie, A* (Sarillo), 146
snowplow parenting, 121–22, 153–54
social media, 183–86
social proficiency. *See* people skills
social skills. *See* people skills; serving
        others
*socialsklz:-) (Social Skills) for Success* (de
        Muyshondt), 186
Spoltore, Sheree, 191–92, 193
Strange Situation, 113–14
structured activity
    overstructuring children, 5–6
    pros and cons of, 49–50
    *See also* unstructured experiences
studies. *See* research studies
summer jobs, 149–50
    *See also* volunteer activities

teenage years
    emotions and responses, 196
    family dinners, impact of, 181–82
    influences, integrating in, 71
    responding to adversity, 90–91
    work opportunities, 149–51
television. *See* media use
"thinking outside the box," 66–67
tiger mom parenting, 87–88

toddler years
  cognitive exploration, 23
  home activities, 26
  museum activities, 24–25
  play needs of toddlers, 32–35
  reading to toddlers, 35
  screen time guidelines, 17–18
  *See also* exploration in children
tolerance and respect, cultivating, 30–32
Tomasello, Michael, 197
Tortolani, Alan, 110–11
Twenge, Jean, 135–36
Tyszka, Tadeusz, 103–4

uninvolved parents, 174
University of California, Davis study,
  92–94
University of Notre Dame study, 90
unstructured experiences
  in entrepreneur's childhood, 48
  value of, 1–3, 49–50
  *See also* free play

"virtual likeability," 183–84

visualization process, 62–63
volunteer activities
  serving others through,
    200–201
  in teen years, 149

Wagner, Tony, 39–40
Walker, Caren, 53
Warneken, Felix, 197
Weissberg, Roger, 168–69
Wells, Kate, 23–24, 25, 26–28, 31
Wetli, Joe, 44–45
"whole-mindedness" concept, 61
Women Innovate Mobile, 45–46
workplaces
  benefits of play in, 34–35
  early work experiences, 148–51
  environment in, 190
  innovation in, 43–45
  "less is more" principle for, 57
  parents, observing in, 145–47

Zao, Hao, 8
Zenger, Jack, 164–65

# ABOUT THE AUTHORS

**Richard Rende, PhD,** is a developmental psychologist, researcher, educator, writer, and consultant. Multiple branches of the National Institutes of Health (NIH) and private foundations have funded his interdisciplinary studies of child development and parenting, resulting in over 200 academic publications, technical papers, and presentations. He has served on numerous editorial boards of leading scientific journals and as a standing member of grant review committees for the NIH/Centers for Scientific Review. The founder of popular blogs on parenting (including the Red-Hot Parenting blog for Parents.com), his work has been featured on NPR, Yahoo!, the *Huffington Post*, the *Wall Street Journal*, Time.com, CNN, MSNBC, and ABC News, and he is author of *Psychosocial Interventions for Genetically Influenced Behavioral Problems in Children and Adolescents*. His educational career has included service on the faculty of the College of Physicians and Surgeons of Columbia University, Rutgers University, and the Alpert Medical School of Brown University. Rende is the Director of Curriculum and Instruction at the Phoenix Country Day School in Paradise Valley, Arizona.

Rende holds a BA from Yale University, an MA from Wesleyan University, and a PhD from Penn State University.

He resides in Paradise Valley, Arizona, with his wife and daughter.

**Jen Prosek** is the founder and CEO of Prosek Partners, a leading international public relations and financial communications consultancy with offices in New York, Connecticut, and London. The firm ranks among the top twenty independent public relations firms in the United States, and among the top five financial communications consultancies in the United States and the United Kingdom. Prosek's first book, *Army of Entrepreneurs*, details the management strategy she used to build Prosek Partners, and offers practical advice to businesses on how to find, train, motivate, and deploy their own army of entrepreneurs within their organizations. Prosek lectures frequently at leading business schools and entrepreneurial and business groups.

Prosek received a BA in English literature from Miami University and her MBA from Columbia University. She is on the board of directors of the Arthur Page Society, BritishAmerican Business, New York City Partnership for the Homeless, and Institute for Public Relations.

She lives in New York City with her husband and daughter.